**Harvard
Business
Review**

on

INCREASING CUSTOMER LOYALTY

The *Harvard Business Review* On series

If you need the best practices and ideas for the business challenges you face—but don't have time to find them—the *Harvard Business Review* **On** series is for you. Each book is a collection of HBR's inspiring and useful perspectives on a specific topic, all in one place. All are available as ebooks, paperbacks, and PDF downloads.

The titles include:

Managing Yourself

HBR on Advancing Your Career
HBR on Succeeding as an Entrepreneur

Managing Others

HBR on Finding & Keeping the Best People
HBR on Inspiring & Executing Innovation
HBR on Winning Negotiations

Managing Your Business

HBR on Aligning Technology with Strategy
HBR on Fixing Health Care from Inside & Out
HBR on Greening Your Business Profitably
HBR on Increasing Customer Loyalty
HBR on Managing Supply Chains
HBR on Rebuilding Your Business Model
HBR on Thriving in Emerging Markets

Harvard Business Review

on

INCREASING CUSTOMER LOYALTY

Harvard Business Review Press

Boston, Massachusetts

Copyright 2011 Harvard Business School Publishing Corporation

All rights reserved

Printed in the United States of America

5 4 3

No part of this publication may be reproduced, stored in or introduced into a retrieval system, or transmitted, in any form, or by any means (electronic, mechanical, photocopying, recording, or otherwise), without the prior permission of the publisher. Requests for permission should be directed to permissions@hbsp.harvard.edu, or mailed to Permissions, Harvard Business School Publishing, 60 Harvard Way, Boston, Massachusetts 02163.

Library of Congress Cataloging-in-Publication Data
Harvard business review on increasing customer loyalty.
    p. cm.—(Harvard business review paperback)
  ISBN 978-1-4221-6252-1 (alk. paper) 1. Customer loyalty.
2. Customer relations. I. Harvard business review.
  HF5415.525.H37 2011
  658.8'343—dc22

                                 2010054387

Contents

**Harvard
Business
Review**

on

INCREASING CUSTOMER LOYALTY

Stop Trying to Delight Your Customers

by Matthew Dixon, Karen Freeman, and Nicholas Toman

THE IDEA THAT COMPANIES must "delight" their customers has become so entrenched that managers rarely examine it. But ask yourself this: How often does someone patronize a company specifically because of its over-the-top service? You can probably think of a few examples, such as the traveler who makes a point of returning to a hotel that has a particularly attentive staff. But you probably can't come up with many.

Now ask yourself: How often do consumers cut companies loose because of terrible service? All the time. They exact revenge on airlines that lose their bags, cable providers whose technicians keep them waiting, cellular companies whose reps put them on permanent hold, and dry cleaners who don't understand what "rush order" means.

Consumers' impulse to punish bad service—at least more readily than to reward delightful service—plays out dramatically in both phone-based and self-service interactions, which are most companies' largest customer service channels. In those settings, our research shows, loyalty has a lot more to do with how well companies deliver on their basic, even plain-vanilla promises than on how dazzling the service experience might be. Yet most companies have failed to realize this and pay dearly in terms of wasted investments and lost customers.

To examine the links between customer service and loyalty, the Customer Contact Council, a division of the Corporate Executive Board, conducted a study of more than 75,000 people who had interacted over the phone with contact-center representatives or through self-service channels such as the web, voice prompts, chat, and e-mail. We also held hundreds of structured interviews with customer service leaders and their functional counterparts in large companies throughout the world. (For more detail, see the sidebar "About the Research.") Our research addressed three questions:

- How important is customer service to loyalty?

- Which customer service activities increase loyalty, and which don't?

- Can companies increase loyalty without raising their customer service operating costs?

Two critical findings emerged that should affect every company's customer service strategy. First, delighting

Idea in Brief

The notion that companies must go above and beyond in their customer service activities is so entrenched that managers rarely examine it. But a study of more than 75,000 people interacting with contact center representatives or using self-service channels found that over-the-top efforts make little difference: All customers really want is a simple, quick solution to their problem. The Corporate Executive Board's Dixon and colleagues describe five loyalty-building tactics that every company should adopt: Reduce the need for repeat calls by anticipating and dealing with related downstream issues; arm reps to address the emotional side of customer interactions; minimize the need for customers to switch service channels; elicit and use feedback from disgruntled or struggling customers; and focus on problem solving, not speed. The authors also introduce the Customer Effort Score and show that it is a better predictor of loyalty than customer satisfaction measures or the Net Promoter Score. And they make available to readers a related diagnostic tool, the Customer Effort Audit. They conclude that we are reaching a tipping point that may presage the end of the telephone as the main channel for service interactions—and that managers therefore have an opportunity to rebuild their service organizations and put reducing customer effort firmly at the core, where it belongs.

customers doesn't build loyalty; reducing their effort— the work they must do to get their problem solved— does. Second, acting deliberately on this insight can help improve customer service, reduce customer service costs, and decrease customer churn.

Trying Too Hard

According to conventional wisdom, customers are more loyal to firms that go above and beyond. But our research shows that exceeding their expectations during service

About the Research

WE DEFINED "LOYALTY" AS CUSTOMERS' intention to continue doing business with a company, increase their spending, or say good things about it (or refrain from saying bad things). During a three-year period, we surveyed more than 75,000 B2C and B2B customers about their recent service interactions in major non-face-to-face channels, including live phone calls, voice prompts, web, chat, and e-mail. The companies represent dozens of industries, ranging from consumer electronics and packaged goods to banking and travel and leisure, in North America, Europe, South Africa, Australia, and New Zealand. We isolated the elements of each interaction that drove customer loyalty, both positively and negatively, and controlled for variables including the type of service issue, whether it was handled by an in-house or an outside contact center, the rep's tenure with the company, the company's size, the customer's personality type, the customer's mood prior to the interaction, switching costs, the frequency with which ads were seen or heard, the perceived product quality and value, product price, the industry, and the specific company. Finally, we conducted several hundred structured interviews in order to understand companies' customer service strategies and operations in detail.

Although our research focused exclusively on contact-center interactions, it makes intuitive sense that the findings apply to face-to-face encounters as well.

interactions (for example, by offering a refund, a free product, or a free service such as expedited shipping) makes customers only marginally more loyal than simply meeting their needs.

For leaders who cut their teeth in the service department, this is an alarming finding. What contact center doesn't have a wall plastered with letters and e-mails from customers praising the extra work that service reps went to on their behalf? Indeed, 89 of the 100 customer service heads we surveyed said that their main strategy is to exceed expectations. But despite these Herculean—and costly—efforts, 84% of customers told us that their expectations had not been exceeded during their most recent interaction.

One reason for the focus on exceeding expectations is that fully 80% of customer service organizations use customer satisfaction (CSAT) scores as the primary metric for gauging the customer's experience. And managers often assume that the more satisfied customers are, the more loyal they will be. But, like others before us (most notably Fred Reichheld), we find little relationship between satisfaction and loyalty. Twenty percent of the "satisfied" customers in our study said they intended to leave the company in question; 28% of the "dissatisfied" customers intended to stay.

The picture gets bleaker still. Although customer service can do little to increase loyalty, it can (and typically does) do a great deal to undermine it. Customers are four times more likely to leave a service interaction disloyal than loyal.

Another way to think about the sources of customer loyalty is to imagine two pies—one containing things that drive loyalty and the other containing things that drive disloyalty. The loyalty pie consists largely of slices such as product quality and brand; the slice for service is quite small. But service accounts for most of the disloyalty pie. We buy from a company because it delivers quality products, great value, or a compelling brand. We leave one, more often than not, because it fails to deliver on customer service.

Make It Easy

Let's return to the key implication of our research: When it comes to service, companies create loyal customers primarily by helping them solve their problems quickly and easily. Armed with this understanding, we can fundamentally change the emphasis of customer service interactions. Framing the service challenge in terms of making it easy for the customer can be highly illuminating, even liberating, especially for companies that have been struggling to delight. Telling frontline reps to exceed customers' expectations is apt to yield confusion, wasted time and effort, and costly giveaways. Telling them to "make it easy" gives them a solid foundation for action.

What exactly does "make it easy" mean? Simply: Remove obstacles. We identified several recurring complaints about service interactions, including three that focus specifically on customer effort. Customers resent having to contact the company repeatedly (or be transferred) to get an issue resolved, having to repeat information, and having to switch from one service channel to another (for instance, needing to call after trying unsuccessfully to solve a problem through the website). Well over half the customers we surveyed reported encountering difficulties of this sort. Companies can reduce these types of effort and measure the effects with a new metric, the Customer Effort Score (CES), which assigns ratings from 1 to 5, with 5 representing very high effort. (For details, see the sidebar "Introducing the Customer Effort Score.")

During our study, we saw many companies that had successfully implemented low-customer-effort approaches to service. Following are five of the tactics they used—tactics that every company should adopt.

1. Don't just resolve the current issue—head off the next one

By far the biggest cause of excessive customer effort is the need to call back. Many companies believe they're performing well in this regard, because they have strong first-contact-resolution (FCR) scores. (See the sidebar "What Should You Measure?") However, 22% of repeat calls involve downstream issues related to the problem that prompted the original call, even if that problem itself was adequately addressed the first time around. Although companies are well equipped to anticipate and "forward-resolve" these issues, they rarely do so, generally because they're overly focused on managing call time. They need to realize that customers gauge the effort they expend not just in terms of how an individual call is handled but also according to how the company manages evolving service events, such as taking out a mortgage or setting up cable service, that typically require several calls.

Bell Canada met this challenge by mining its customer interaction data to understand the relationships among various customer issues. Using what it learned about "event clusters," Bell began training its reps not

What Should You Measure?

THE NUMBER ONE CAUSE of undue effort for customers interacting with contact centers is the need to call back because their issue wasn't resolved on the first attempt.

Companies trying to measure how well reps resolve issues in a single call typically use the first-contact-resolution (FCR) metric, but fully half the time that doesn't supply information about repeat calls and the reasons behind them. Tracking repeat calls within a specified period (we recommend seven to 14 days) is not only easier than measuring FCR but also casts a wider net, capturing the implicit, or nonobvious, reasons customers call back, such as related downstream issues or an emotional disconnect with a rep. A word of caution: Tracking repeat calls instead of using FCR inevitably makes performance appear worse. However, we believe that it is a far better way to spot and eliminate sources of undue customer effort and that it can help companies boost loyalty in ways FCR cannot.

only to resolve the customer's primary issue but also to anticipate and address common downstream issues. For instance, a high percentage of customers who ordered a particular feature called back for instructions on using it. The company's service reps now give a quick tutorial to customers about key aspects of the feature before hanging up. This sort of forward resolution enabled Bell to reduce its "calls per event" by 16% and its customer churn by 6%. For complex downstream issues that would take excessive time to address in the initial call, the company sends follow-up e-mails—for example, explaining how to interpret the first billing statement. Bell Canada is currently weaving this issue-prediction approach into the call-routing experience for the customer.

Fidelity uses a similar concept on its self-service website, offering "suggested next steps" to customers executing certain transactions. Often customers who change their address online call later to order new checks or ask about homeowners' or renters' insurance; therefore, Fidelity directs them to these topics before they leave the site. Twenty-five percent of all self-service transactions on Fidelity's website are now generated by similar "next issue" prompts, and calls per household have dropped by 5% since the policy began.

2. Arm reps to address the emotional side of customer interactions

Twenty-four percent of the repeat calls in our study stemmed from emotional disconnects between customers and reps—situations in which, for instance, the customer didn't trust the rep's information or didn't like the answer given and had the impression that the rep was just hiding behind general company policy. With some basic instruction, reps can eliminate many interpersonal issues and thereby reduce repeat calls.

One UK-based mortgage company teaches its reps how to listen for clues to a customer's personality type. They quickly assess whether they are talking to a "controller," a "thinker," a "feeler," or an "entertainer," and tailor their responses accordingly, offering the customer the balance of detail and speed appropriate for the personality type diagnosed. This strategy has reduced repeat calls by a remarkable 40%.

Introducing the Customer Effort Score

WE EVALUATED THE PREDICTIVE POWER of three metrics—customer satisfaction (CSAT), the Net Promoter Score (NPS), and a new metric we developed, the Customer Effort Score (CES)—on customer loyalty, defined as customers' intention to keep doing business with the company, increase the amount they spend, or spread positive (and not negative) word of mouth. Not surprisingly, CSAT was a poor predictor. NPS proved better (and has been shown to be a powerful gauge at the company level). CES outperformed both in customer service interactions.

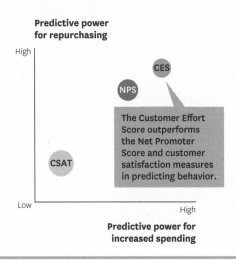

Predictive power for repurchasing

High

CES

NPS

The Customer Effort Score outperforms the Net Promoter Score and customer satisfaction measures in predicting behavior.

CSAT

Low   High

Predictive power for increased spending

The lighting company Osram Sylvania sifts through its call transcripts to pinpoint words that tend to trigger negative reactions and drive repeat calls—words like "can't," "won't," and "don't"—and coaches its reps on alternate phrasing. Instead of saying "We don't have that item in stock," a rep might explain, "We'll have stock availability for that item in two weeks." Through such simple changes in language, Osram Sylvania has

CES is measured by asking a single question: "How much effort did you personally have to put forth to handle your request?" It is scored on a scale from 1 (very low effort) to 5 (very high effort). Customer service organizations can use CES, along with operational measurements of such things as repeat calls, transfers, and channel switching, to conduct an "effort audit" and improve areas where customers are expending undue energy. Many of the companies we work with use CES to intervene with customers at risk of defecting.

We found the predictive power of CES to be strong indeed. Of the customers who reported low effort, 94% expressed an intention to repurchase, and 88% said they would increase their spending. Only 1% said they would speak negatively about the company. Conversely, 81% of the customers who had a hard time solving their problems reported an intention to spread negative word of mouth.

We believe that the superior performance of CES in the service environment derives from two factors: its ability to capture customer impressions at the transactional level (as opposed to NPS, which captures more holistic impressions of a company) and its ability to capture negative experiences as well as positive ones.

A related diagnostic tool, the Customer Effort Audit, can be downloaded at http://www.executiveboard.com/salesandmarketing/CCC-CustomerEffortAudit.html.

lowered its Customer Effort Score from 2.8 to 2.2—18.5% below the average we see for B2B companies.

LoyaltyOne, the operator of the AIR MILES reward program, teaches reps to probe for information they can use to better position potentially disappointing outcomes. A rep dealing with a customer who wants to redeem miles for an unavailable flight might learn that the caller is traveling to an important business meeting

Obstacles All Too Common

MOST CUSTOMERS ENCOUNTER loyalty-eroding problems when they engage with customer service:

56% report having to re-explain an issue

57% report having to switch from the web to the phone

59% report expending moderate-to-high effort to resolve an issue

59% report being transferred

62% report having to repeatedly contact the company to resolve an issue

---

and use this fact to put a positive spin on the need to book a different flight. The rep might say, "It sounds like this is something you can't be late for. The Monday morning flight isn't available, but with potential delays, you'd be cutting it close anyway. I'd recommend a Sunday evening flight so that you don't risk missing your meeting." This strategy has resulted in an 11% decrease in repeat contacts.

3. Minimize channel switching by increasing self-service channel "stickiness."

Many companies ask, "How can we get our customers to go to our self-service website?" Our research shows that in fact many customers have already been there: Fifty-seven percent of inbound calls came from customers who went to the website first. Despite their desire to have customers turn to the web, companies tend to resist making improvements to their sites, assuming that only heavy spending and technology upgrades will

The Bad-Service Ripple Effect

SERVICE FAILURES NOT ONLY drive existing customers to defect—they also can repel prospective ones. Our research shows:

25% of customers are likely to say something positive about their customer service experience

65% are likely to speak negatively

23% of customers who had a positive service interaction told 10 or more people about it

48% of customers who had negative experiences told 10 or more others

---

induce customers to stay there. (And even when costly upgrades are made, they often prove counterproductive, because companies tend to add complicated and confusing features in an attempt to keep up with their competitors.)

Customers may become overwhelmed by the profusion of self-service channels—interactive voice response, websites, e-mail, chat, online support communities, social media such as Facebook and Twitter, and so on—and often lack the ability to make the best choice for themselves. For example, technically unsophisticated users, left to their own devices, may go to highly technical online support communities. As a result, customers may expend a lot of effort bouncing between channels, only to pick up the phone in the end.

Cisco Consumer Products now guides customers to the channel it determines will suit them best, on the basis of segment-specific hypotheses generated by the company's customer experience team. Language on the site's home page nudges technology gurus toward the online support community; those with less technical expertise are steered toward knowledge articles by the promise of simple step-by-step instructions. The company eliminated the e-mail option, having found that it didn't reliably reduce customer effort. (Our research shows that 2.4 e-mails, on average, are needed to resolve an issue, compared with 1.7 calls.) When Cisco Consumer Products began this program, in 2006, only 30% of its customer contacts were handled through self-service; the figure today is 84%, and the volume of calls has dropped accordingly.

Travelocity reduced customer effort just by improving the help section of its website. It had learned that many customers who sought solutions there were stymied and resorted to the phone. By eliminating jargon, simplifying the layout, and otherwise improving readability, the company doubled the use of its "top searches" and decreased calls by 5%.

4. Use feedback from disgruntled or struggling customers to reduce customer effort

Many companies conduct postcall surveys to measure internal performance; however, they may neglect to use the data they collect to learn from unhappy customers. But consider National Australia Group's approach. The company has frontline reps specifically trained to call customers who have given it low marks. The reps focus first on resolving the customers' issues, but they also collect feedback that informs service improvements. The company's issue-resolution rate has risen by 31%.

Such learning and intervention isn't limited to the phone channel. Some companies monitor online behavior in order to identify customers who are struggling. EarthLink has a dedicated team of reps who step in as needed with clients on its self-service website—for example, by initiating a chat with a customer who has spent more than 90 seconds in the knowledge center or clicked on the "Contact Us" link. This program has reduced calls by 8%.

5. Empower the front line to deliver a low-effort experience

Incentive systems that value speed over quality may pose the single greatest barrier to reducing customer effort. Most customer service organizations still emphasize productivity metrics such as average handle time when assessing rep performance. They would be better off removing the productivity "governors" that get in the way of making the customer's experience easy.

An Australian telecommunications provider eliminated all productivity metrics from its frontline reps' performance scorecards. Although handle time increased slightly, repeat calls fell by 58%. Today the company evaluates its reps solely on the basis of short, direct interviews with customers, essentially asking them if the service they received met their needs.

Freed to focus on reducing customer effort, frontline reps can easily pick low-hanging fruit. Ameriprise Financial, for example, asks its customer service reps to capture every instance in which they are forced to tell a customer no. While auditing the "no's," the company found many legacy policies that had been outmoded by regulatory changes or system or process improvements. During its first year of "capturing the no's," Ameriprise modified or eliminated 26 policies. It has since expanded the program by asking frontline reps to come up with other process efficiencies, generating $1.2 million in savings as a result.

Some companies have gone even further, making low customer effort the cornerstone of their service value proposition and branding. South Africa's Nedbank, for instance, instituted an "AskOnce" promise, which guarantees that the rep who picks up the phone will own the customer's issue from start to finish.

––––––––––––

The immediate mission is clear: Corporate leaders must focus their service organizations on mitigating disloyalty by reducing customer effort. But service managers fretting about how to reengineer their contact centers— departments built on a foundation of delighting the customer—should consider this: A massive shift is under way in terms of customers' service preferences. Although most companies believe that customers overwhelmingly prefer live phone service to self-service, our most recent data show that customers are, in fact, indifferent. This is an important tipping point and probably presages the end of phone-based service as the primary channel for customer service interactions. For enterprising service managers, it presents an opportunity to rebuild their organizations around self-service and, in the process, to put reducing customer effort firmly at the core, where it belongs.

MATTHEW DIXON is the managing director of the Corporate Executive Board's Sales and Service Practice. **KAREN FREEMAN** is the research director of the Sales Executive Council, and **NICHOLAS TOMAN** is the research director of the Customer Contact Council, both divisions of the Corporate Executive Board's Sales and Service Practice.

Originally published in July 2010. Reprint R1007L

Companies and the Customers Who Hate Them

by Gail McGovern and Youngme Moon

ONE OF THE MOST INFLUENTIAL propositions in marketing is that customer satisfaction begets loyalty, and loyalty begets profits. Why, then, do so many companies infuriate their customers by binding them with contracts, bleeding them with fees, confounding them with fine print, and otherwise penalizing them for their business? Because, unfortunately, it pays. Companies have found that confused and ill-informed customers, who often end up making poor purchasing decisions, can be highly profitable indeed.

What follows is a cautionary tale. Some companies consciously and cynically exploit customers in this way. But in our conversations with dozens of executives in various industries, we found that the majority of firms that profit from their customers' confusion have unwittingly fallen into a trap. Without ever making a deliberate decision to do so, they have, over a period of years, taken greater advantage of their customers. In most cases, there's no defining moment when these companies crossed the line. Rather, they found themselves on a slippery slope that led to an increasingly antagonistic strategy.

Think of the cell phone service, banking, and credit card industries, each of which now demonstrably profits from customers who fail to understand or follow the rules about minute use, minimum balances, overdrafts, credit limits, or payment deadlines. Most of the companies in these industries started out with product and pricing strategies designed to provide value to a variety of customer segments, each with its own needs and price sensitivities.

Yet today, many companies in these industries and others find that their transparent, customer-centric strategies for delivering value have evolved into opaque, company-centric strategies for extracting it. Although this approach may work for a while—many notable practitioners are highly profitable—businesses that prey on customers are perpetually vulnerable to their pent-up hostility. At any time, customers may retaliate with vitriol, lawsuits, and defection.

Companies that extract value as a conscious strategy know who they are. But for those that do not realize where they're headed, this article can help them recognize and dismantle these risky value-extracting practices, reducing their vulnerability to customer retaliation and increasing their competitive advantage.

Idea in Brief

A company's most profitable customers may be those who make the worst purchasing decisions. Consider retail banking. Depending on the minimum balance consumers agree to keep in their accounts, banks set particular interest rates and fees. If a customer's balance falls below the minimum, he pays penalties. If it climbs well above the minimum, he's stuck with a low interest rate. Either way, the bank wins; the customer loses.

Firms taking advantage of customers through such tactics, whether deliberate or unintentional, trigger a backlash: consumers retaliate—with lawsuits, mass defections, and company-specific "hate sites."

How to avoid enraging customers? Identify and eradicate practices that *extract* value from them, advise McGovern and Moon. Then adopt practices that *provide* value to customers. For example, online bank ING Direct offers accounts with no minimums or tiered interest rates—and has become the nation's fourth-largest thrift bank.

The Slippery Slope

Companies can profit from customers' confusion, ignorance, and poor decision making in two related ways. The first evolves out of the legitimate attempt to create value by giving customers a broad set of offerings. The second emerges from the equally legitimate decision to use fees and penalties to cover costs and discourage undesirable customer behavior.

In the first case, a company creates a diverse product and pricing portfolio to offer various value propositions to different customer segments. All else being equal, a hotel that has three types of rooms at three price points can serve a wider customer base than a hotel that has just one type of room at one price. However, customers

Idea in Practice

McGovern and Moon offer these guidelines for replacing company-centric with customer-centric policies.

Recognize Company-Centric Strategies

Adversarial value-extracting strategies are common across industries. Recognizing these strategies can help you avoid them in your own firm.

Example: Cell phone service carriers offer several dozen pricing options. They then take advantage of customers' difficulty in predicting their usage by penalizing them for using too much time or not enough time. Fifty percent of U.S. carriers' income derives from such fees.

Health clubs' most profitable customers are those who have been enticed to sign up for a long-term membership but who then rarely visit the club. Knowing this, many clubs intentionally sell far more memberships than they have the floor space to accommodate. And through confusing contractual language, they make it difficult for customers to extricate themselves from the deal.

Look for Warning Signs

To spot signs of harmful practices in your company, ask:

- **Are our most profitable customers those who have the most reason to be dissatisfied with us?** If yes, it's a matter of time before your customers will retaliate.

- **Do we have rules we want customers to break because doing so generates profits?** Rules that, if violated by a

benefit from such diversity only when they are guided toward the offering that best suits their needs. A company is less likely to help customers make good choices if it knows that it can generate more profits when they make poor ones.

Of course, only the most flagrant companies would explicitly seduce customers into making bad choices. Yet there are subtle ways in which even generally well-intentioned firms use complex portfolios to encourage customer, preserve or enhance value for your firm are actually mechanisms for taking advantage of customers.

- **Do we make it hard for customers to understand or abide by our rules?** Certain cell phone carriers, for example, make it cumbersome for customers to monitor their minute use.

- **Do we depend on contracts to prevent customers from defecting?** When companies use long-term contracts merely to prevent poorly served but profitable customers from defecting, they're demonstrating a lack of confidence in their value proposition.

Put Customers First

Sometimes all it takes to trigger a mass defection from a company-centric firm is the appearance of a customer-friendly competitor—one that puts customer satisfaction and transparency first.

Example: Virgin Mobile USA offers a pay-as-you-go pricing plan with no hidden fees, no time-of-day restrictions, no contracts, and straightforward, reasonable rates. It has nearly five million subscribers and a customer churn rate well below the industry average. Customer satisfaction hovers in the 90th percentile. And more than two-thirds of customers reported recommending Virgin to friends and family.

suboptimal choices—tactics that hasten the descent down the slippery slope. Complicated offerings can confuse customers with a lack of transparency (hotels, for example, often don't reveal information about discounts and upgrades); they can make it hard for customers to distinguish among products, even when complete information is available (as is often the case with banking services); and they can take advantage of consumers' difficulty in predicting their needs (for instance, how many cell phone minutes they'll use each month).

Companies can also profit from customers' bad decisions by overrelying on penalties and fees. Such charges may have been conceived as a way to deter undesirable customer behavior and offset the costs that businesses incur as a result of that behavior. Penalties for bouncing a check, for example, were originally designed to discourage banking customers from spending more than they had and to recoup administrative costs. The practice was thus fair to company and customer alike. But many firms have discovered just how profitable penalties can be; as a result, they have an incentive to encourage their customers to incur them—or, at least, not to discourage them from doing so. Many credit card issuers, for example, choose not to deny a transaction that would put the cardholder over his or her credit limit; it's more profitable to let the customer overspend and then impose penalties.

The Strategies at Work

These adversarial value-extracting strategies are common across industries, from banking and hotels to video stores, book-purchasing clubs, ticketing agencies, and car rentals. Here we'll look in detail at some examples of these strategies in the cell phone service, retail-banking, and health club industries.

Cell Phone Service Industry
When they sign up for service plans, cell phone customers must generally choose a pricing "bucket." A typical

carrier, for example, offers several dozen pricing options, ranging from low-priced plans that come with a limited number of minutes to high-priced plans that come with thousands. Each plan has its own restrictions and allowances.

While this may appear to be a customer-centric way of offering value, these service portfolios are in essence designed to take advantage of customers' difficulty in predicting their usage by penalizing them either for using too much time or for not using enough. The carrier benefits when consumers choose plans that don't reflect their actual consumption patterns, regardless of the direction of the error. In fact, as much as 50% of U.S. carriers' income comes from overage and underage fees—what the industry refers to as "breakage."

Tactics like these may be profitable, but they also fuel seething discontent. The U.S. Federal Communications Commission logs tens of thousands of consumer complaints against cell phone companies per year. The constant carping, which proliferates on blogs and company-specific hate sites (www.hateverizon.org is a typical example), generates untold amounts of bad publicity. Deep dissatisfaction is further manifest in relentless customer churn; it is not unusual, for example, for a major carrier to turn over a quarter of its customer base in a year—a strikingly high percentage, given that most users are shackled by contracts. This level of turnover requires companies to engage in endless, aggressive customer acquisition, including extravagant spending on advertising. In 2005, the U.S. cell phone service industry spent more than $6 billion on ads, with acquisition costs averaging $300 to $400 per customer.

Dissatisfaction and churn should be particularly worrisome to firms that see their customers defecting to a competitor that provides a transparent and friendly alternative. Consider what happened in the cell phone industry when Virgin Mobile USA arrived on the scene in 2002. The deck seemed to be stacked firmly against the company: The industry was already crowded, penetration was high, revenue growth was slowing, and Virgin enjoyed little U.S. brand recognition, aside from its reputation as a quirky airline.

What the company did have going for it was its simple offer: a pay-as-you-go pricing plan with no hidden fees, no time-of-day restrictions, no contracts, and straightforward, reasonable rates. With an annual advertising budget of only $50 million (less than one-tenth the budget of some incumbents), the company acquired 1 million subscribers in five quarters, matching the industry record for reaching that mark.

Today, Virgin Mobile USA has nearly 5 million subscribers and a churn rate well below the industry average for pay-as-you-go subscriptions, even though its customers are free to leave without penalty. In an industry notorious for low satisfaction rates, Virgin's customer satisfaction has been stellar, hovering in the 90th percentile since the service launched. What's more, existing customers have been acting as goodwill ambassadors: As of last year, more than two-thirds reported recommending the service to friends and family.

Virgin's competitive strategy was explicitly designed to take advantage of customers' unhappiness with the abusive practices of incumbents. As Dan Schulman, CEO of Virgin Mobile USA, told us, "Our target customers didn't trust the industry pricing plans. These are savvy consumers, and they hate feeling like they're being conned. We designed an offer to differentiate ourselves from the competition." Schulman's remarks echo comments we heard from executives in the banking, health club, and mutual fund industries, among others, who have designed transparent offers as a conscious strategy to attract their rivals' dissatisfied customers.

Retail-Banking Industry

When people sign up for checking accounts, they are usually asked to choose from more than a dozen offerings. Depending on the minimum balance they agree to keep in the account, the bank pays a particular interest rate and may waive or adjust certain fees.

But consider what happens if customers do not stay within their minimum balance buckets. If their balances fall below the minimum, they pay various penalties and service charges; if their balances climb well above the minimum, they are stuck with a lower interest rate than they would have earned had they chosen a different bucket. Here again, the firm wins and customers lose, regardless of the direction of the error. And here again, customers who make unwise product selections tend to be more profitable than those whose selections fit their needs.

As banks have discovered the profit potential of fees and penalties, they have gradually adjusted their tactics to take advantage of customers. When some banks tally up customers' accounts at the end of each day, for example, they debit checks in order of size—biggest check first—rather than chronologically. This increases the chance that the remaining checks will bounce, allowing the bank to charge the customer for multiple overdrafts. Similarly, many banks have phased in "courtesy" overdraft provisions that enhance the likelihood that customers will engage in consumption behaviors resulting in penalties. Customers using ATMs, for example, are increasingly allowed to overcharge their accounts without being informed that they are doing so; notification comes later, in the form of a hefty penalty.

According to one estimate, consumers paid $53 billion in overdraft fees in 2006, a 58% increase from five years earlier. These numbers are only rising: The average overdraft fee hit a record high in 2006. Overall fees levied on customer accounts have climbed steadily during the past decade; in 2005, increases in fee income at four of the ten largest banks were in the double digits.

On the face of it, milking consumers for fees would seem to be an effective business strategy. Profits for American banks have increased by close to 67% over the past ten years. Stock prices are up for the largest banks, and so are revenues. So why shouldn't banks rely on high fees? As in the case of the cell phone industry, customer frustration has become acute. According to a recent Consumer Federation of America survey, an overwhelming majority of people believe

---

☐ Are your most profitable customers those who have the most reason to be dissatisfied with you?

☐ Do you have rules that you want customers to break because doing so generates profits?

☐ Do you make it difficult for customers to understand or abide by your rules, and do you actually help customers break them?

☐ Do you depend on contracts to prevent customers from defecting?

---

that permitting overdrafts without notice constitutes an unfair business practice. Consumer complaints have become so pervasive that in 2007, New York congresswoman Carolyn Maloney reintroduced the Consumer Overdraft Protection Fair Practices Act to prevent banks from charging overdraft protection fees unless customers explicitly opt in to the service.

These banking practices have a powerfully corrosive effect on customer satisfaction. Consumers haven't been shy about using the legal system to express their ire. Bank of America, for instance, is fighting a much-publicized class action lawsuit alleging that the bank improperly collected overdraft fees from direct deposit accounts configured to receive Social Security benefits.

It's no surprise that when a nice guy comes along, customers defect. Consider the online bank ING Direct: In the six years since its launch, ING Direct has taken a determinedly customer-friendly stance, offering products that are straightforward and easy to understand. From the start, the firm deliberately rejected banking orthodoxy by offering savings accounts with no fees, no tiered interest rates, and no minimums. Today, it offers equally simple checking accounts and gives customers surcharge-free access to a network of ATMs. Its Web site contains none of the cross-selling clutter that is characteristic of most banking sites, and its portfolio of offerings remains a paragon of product and pricing simplicity.

The approach has paid off. ING Direct is now the fourth-largest thrift bank in the United States, with total assets of more than $60 billion. In this highly competitive industry, ING Direct is adding 100,000 new customers a month, and its customer base is rapidly approaching 5 million.

Health Club Industry

Health club companies have a long history of luring customers with attractive short-term offers, assaulting them with aggressive sales pitches, and then binding them with long-term contracts. That's because some of their most profitable customers on a cost-to-serve basis have been those who were enticed to sign up for a long-term membership but then rarely visited the club. Indeed, many companies, knowing that the typical health club customer will underuse the facility, intentionally sell many more memberships than they have the floor space to accommodate.

Moreover, many health clubs make it hard for customers to understand the terms of the contract and figure out the options for extricating themselves from the agreements. An investigation conducted by the New York City Council a few years ago, for example, concluded that 41% of clubs in the city didn't explain their fees in writing, 81% didn't give potential members a contract to read at home, and 96% didn't inform customers of all the ways they could legally cancel a contract.

Not surprisingly, many of these firms have faced the same customer wrath that has plagued the cell phone and banking industries. In New York State, hundreds of formal complaints led then attorney general Eliot Spitzer to launch an investigation in 2001 into the sales and marketing practices of Bally Total Fitness, the industry's largest player. The firm settled in 2004, agreeing to improve its cancellation policies, monitor compliance with them, and make restitution to customers. The state of New Jersey, also responding to hundreds of complaints, has brought litigation against almost two dozen health clubs that allegedly failed to notify customers of their rights or provided fraudulent contracts. The U.S. Better Business Bureau continues to receive thousands of complaints per year about health clubs, putting the industry in the top 1% for the volume of complaints received.

Customer churn at the major health clubs continues unabated, running as high as 40% annually despite the lock-in demanded by contracts. Endemic customer dissatisfaction has put health clubs on a customer-acquisition treadmill that requires them to spend ever more to attract new customers as their existing ones seek a way out.

The industry appears ripe for an existing player to break ranks or for a new one to challenge the industry's bad behavior. In fact, some clubs seem to be getting the idea. Life Time Fitness has become one of the largest fitness chains in the country by eschewing contracts altogether. Membership to Life Time Fitness comes with a 30-day money-back guarantee and can be canceled at any time with no penalty. The company's attrition rate is 10% below the industry average, even though its customers can easily leave. Meanwhile, other clubs—including Curves, 24 Hour Fitness, and a host of smaller companies—are now offering pay-as-you-go options and experimenting with less antagonistic, even encouraging, ways to retain customers, such as reward points for members who work out regularly. As Brad Fogel, chief marketing officer at 24 Hour Fitness, explains, "We've learned that by giving customers incentives to visit the club more frequently, they become more loyal and ultimately remain with us longer."

Although these clubs cater to different segments (Life Time Fitness, for example, attracts families looking for a lavish array of services, while Curves is known for its no-frills, bare-bones workout facilities), they share an explicit strategy of attracting customers disillusioned with the aggressive, acquisition-oriented approach for which the industry is known.

The Warning Signs

In our research, we've talked with executives from industries that, to a greater or lesser degree, profit from confused or ill-informed customers who make poor purchasing decisions. We've also identified a number of industries in which firms are just starting down the slippery slope as they discover the short-term profit potential of hidden fees, mysterious surcharges, confusing service options, and tricky fine print. This trend is apparent in the rental car industry, for example, as well as in the entertainment ticketing industry, where service, convenience, order processing, restoration, and other fees can add 10% to the base price of a ticket.

In almost every case, the executives we've spoken to have expressed discomfort with the practices, acknowledging them but arguing that they don't represent an intentional strategy. Almost uniformly, they describe a largely unconscious process of uncoordinated implementation. The punitive fees and restrictive contracts evolved gradually, with each value-extracting addition only slightly more company centric than the one that preceded it. As a result, these executives now find themselves conducting business in ways that they know make them vulnerable and create opportunities for competitors. But having slid this far down the slope, they find it hard to get a purchase on the way back up.

Companies should be on the lookout for signs of these harmful practices. As a start, executives should ask themselves the following four questions.

Are our most profitable customers those who have the most reason to be dissatisfied with us?

If the answer is yes, the company is extracting value from customers who do not feel they're getting a fair return and, in the process, exposing itself to a range of risks. A yes answer doesn't mean that customers are up in arms—yet. Rather, it means that they're not receiving the value they're paying for. It's only a matter of time before they look for ways to retaliate: at best, by spreading bad word of mouth—at worst, by suing and defecting.

Do we have rules we want customers to break because doing so generates profits?
There are certainly situations in which it is reasonable for a firm to penalize a customer—for instance, if a hotel guest destroys property. The penalty exists to recover costs, protect value for other customers, and, one hopes, act as a deterrent. However, when a company institutes a rule that, if violated, destroys value neither for the firm nor for its other customers, that rule will in time be recognized for what it is: a mechanism allowing the firm to extract additional value from customers. Such is the case when a bank charges a customer for conducting more than an allotted number of ATM transactions.

Do we make it difficult for customers to understand or abide by our rules, and do we actually help customers break them?
Companies should examine whether they actively facilitate profitable "bad" customer behaviors—things like bouncing checks, returning videos late, and exceeding credit card and cell-phone-minute limits. (Certain carriers, for example, make it cumbersome for customers to monitor their minute use.) Companies should also examine their product portfolios to determine whether their diverse offerings are designed to

provide value or to take advantage of customers' ignorance or difficulty in choosing options that are in their
best interest.

Do we depend on contracts to prevent customers from defecting?

Some situations clearly call for contracts just as some call
for penalties. A manufacturer should not sell a $5 million
mainframe computer on a handshake, for example.
However, when contracts are used merely to prevent
poorly served but profitable customers from defecting,
they can harm both customer and provider.

Companies that rely on service contracts should ask
whether these are functioning as the opposite of service
guarantees. A service guarantee tells customers that the
company is so confident in the quality of its value
proposition that it will compensate customers who are
not satisfied. In contrast, a long-term contract indicates
that the company lacks confidence in its value proposition and needs to lock customers in so that it can keep
their money even if they become dissatisfied. When
such contracts are considered to be critical to a company's profitability or financial viability, it's a sign that
the firm may be extracting value at the expense of customer satisfaction.

Climbing Back into Favor

Great CEOs recognize and seize opportunities;
they also identify and eliminate vulnerabilities. The
company-centric strategies described here represent a

vulnerability—and any CEO focused on long-term sustainability would be wise to identify these strategies in the firm and begin dismantling them. Clearly, such practices can work in the short term, as the profits of certain practitioners attest. But as competitors emerge to exploit consumers' pent-up hostility, companies that bleed their customers in the ways described here should expect a punishing response, sooner or later.

As we've seen, sometimes all it takes to drive a mass defection is the appearance of a customer-friendly competitor: a firm that puts customer satisfaction and transparency first. The video rental industry learned the lesson the hard way when its customers, infuriated by late fees, flocked to service-oriented, fee-free Netflix when it launched in 1997. Netflix, it should be noted, had early success with its customer-friendly strategy but then landed on the slippery slope itself; a recent class action lawsuit against the company alleged that it intentionally delayed disc delivery to its heaviest users, thereby penalizing its best customers. The company has since taken steps to ensure that its method of prioritizing customer demand—based on what it considers a "fairness algorithm"—is more transparent.

Risk reduction is a good reason to purge antagonistic value-extracting practices. But doing so also presents companies with an opportunity for competitive differentiation. In industries where squeezing value from customers is commonplace, a transparent, value-creating offer can exploit customers' dissatisfaction with incumbents and drive rapid growth.

GAIL MCGOVERN is a professor of management practice and **YOUNGME MOON** is an associate professor of business administration at Harvard Business School.

Originally published in June 2007. Reprint R0706E

The One Number You Need to Grow

by Frederick F. Reichheld

THE CEOS IN THE ROOM knew all about the power of loyalty. They had already transformed their companies into industry leaders, largely by building intensely loyal relationships with customers and employees. Now the chief executives—from Vanguard, Chick-fil-A, State Farm, and a half-dozen other leading companies—had gathered at a daylong forum to swap insights that would help them further enhance their loyalty efforts. And what they were hearing from Andy Taylor, the CEO of Enterprise Rent-A-Car, was riveting.

Taylor and his senior team had figured out a way to measure and manage customer loyalty without the complexity of traditional customer surveys. Every month, Enterprise polled its customers using just two simple questions, one about the quality of their rental experience and the other about the likelihood that they would rent from the company again. Because the process was so simple, it was fast. That allowed the company to publish ranked results for its 5,000 U.S.

branches within days, giving the offices real-time feed-back on how they were doing and the opportunity to learn from successful peers.

The survey was different in another important way. In ranking the branches, the company counted only the customers who gave the experience the highest possible rating. That narrow focus on enthusiastic customers surprised the CEOs in the room. Hands shot up. What about the rest of Enterprise's customers, the marginally satisfied who continued to rent from Enterprise and were necessary to its business? Wouldn't it be better to track, in a more sophisticated way, mean or median statistics? No, Taylor said. By concentrating solely on those most enthusiastic about their rental experience, the company could focus on a key driver of profitable growth: customers who not only return to rent again but also recommend Enterprise to their friends.

Enterprise's approach surprised me, too. Most customer satisfaction surveys aren't very useful. They tend to be long and complicated, yielding low response rates and ambiguous implications that are difficult for operating managers to act on. Furthermore, they are rarely challenged or audited because most senior executives, board members, and investors don't take them very seriously. That's because their results don't correlate tightly with profits or growth.

But Enterprise's method—and its ability to generate profitable growth through what appeared to be quite a simple tool—got me thinking that the company might be on to something. Could you get similar results in other industries—including those seemingly more

Idea in Brief

Companies spend lots of time and money on complex tools to assess customer satisfaction. But they're measuring the wrong thing. The best predictor of top-line growth can usually be captured in a single survey question: Would you recommend this company to a friend? This finding is based on two years of research in which a variety of survey questions were tested by linking the responses with actual customer behavior—purchasing patterns and referrals—and ultimately with company growth. Surprisingly, the most effective question wasn't about customer satisfaction or even loyalty per se. In most of the industries studied, the percentage of customers enthusiastic enough about a company to refer it to a friend or colleague directly correlated with growth rates among competitors. Willingness to talk up a company or product to friends, family, and colleagues is one of the best indicators of loyalty because of the customer's sacrifice in making the recommendation. When customers act as references, they do more than indicate they've received good economic value from a company; they put their own reputations on the line. The findings point to a new, simpler approach to customer research, one directly linked to a company's results.

complex than car rentals—by focusing only on customers who provided the most enthusiastic responses to a short list of questions designed to assess their loyalty to a company? Could the list be reduced to a single question? If so, what would that question be?

It took me two years of research to figure that out, research that linked survey responses with actual customer behavior—purchasing patterns and referrals—and ultimately with company growth. The results were clear yet counterintuitive. It turned out that a single survey question can, in fact, serve as a useful predictor of growth. But that question isn't about customer satisfaction or even loyalty—at least in so many words. Rather, it's about customers' willingness to recommend a product or service to someone else. In fact, in most of the industries that I studied, the percentage of customers who were enthusiastic enough to refer a friend or colleague—perhaps the strongest sign of customer loyalty—correlated directly with differences in growth rates among competitors.

Certainly, other factors besides customer loyalty play a role in driving a company's growth—economic or industry expansion, innovation, and so on. And I don't want to overstate the findings: Although the "would recommend" question generally proved to be the most effective in determining loyalty and predicting growth, that wasn't the case in every single industry. But evangelistic customer loyalty is clearly one of the most important drivers of growth. While it doesn't guarantee growth, in general, profitable growth can't be achieved without it.

Furthermore, these findings point to an entirely new approach to customer surveys, one based on simplicity that directly links to a company's results. By substituting a single question—blunt tool though it may appear to be—for the complex black box of the typical customer satisfaction survey, companies can actually put consumer survey results to use and focus employees on the task of stimulating growth.

Loyalty and Growth

Before I describe my research and the results from a number of industries, let's briefly look at the concept of loyalty and some of the mistakes companies make when trying to measure it. First, a definition. Loyalty is the willingness of someone—a customer, an employee, a friend—to make an investment or personal sacrifice in order to strengthen a relationship. For a customer, that can mean sticking with a supplier who treats him well and gives him good value in the long term even if the supplier does not offer the best price in a particular transaction.

Consequently, customer loyalty is about much more than repeat purchases. Indeed, even someone who buys again and again from the same company may not necessarily be loyal to that company but instead may be trapped by inertia, indifference, or exit barriers erected by the company or circumstance. (Someone may regularly take the same airline to a city only because it offers the most flights there.) Conversely, a loyal customer may not make frequent repeat purchases because of a reduced need for a product or service. (Someone may buy a new car less often as he gets older and drives less.)

True loyalty clearly affects profitability. While regular customers aren't always profitable, their choice to stick with a product or service typically reduces a company's customer acquisition costs. Loyalty also drives top-line growth. Obviously, no company can grow if its customer bucket is leaky, and loyalty helps eliminate this outflow. Indeed, loyal customers can raise the water level in the bucket: Customers who are truly loyal tend to buy more over time, as their incomes grow or they devote a larger share of their wallets to a company they feel good about.

And loyal customers talk up a company to their friends, family, and colleagues. In fact, such a recommendation is one of the best indicators of loyalty because of the customer's sacrifice, if you will, in making the recommendation. When customers act as references, they do more than indicate that they've received good economic value from a company; they put their own reputations on the line. And they will risk their reputations only if they feel intense loyalty. (Note that here, too, loyalty may have little to do with repeat purchases. As someone's income increases, she may move up the automotive ladder from the Hondas she has bought for years. But if she is loyal to the company, she will enthusiastically recommend a Honda to, say, a nephew who is buying his first car.)

The tendency of loyal customers to bring in new customers—at no charge to the company—is particularly beneficial as a company grows, especially if it operates in a mature industry. In such a case, the tremendous marketing costs of acquiring each new customer through advertising and other promotions make it hard to grow profitably. In fact, the only path to profitable growth may lie in a company's ability to get its loyal customers to become, in effect, its marketing department.

The Wrong Yardsticks

Because loyalty is so important to profitable growth, measuring and managing it make good sense. Unfortunately, existing approaches haven't proved very effective. Not only does their complexity make them practically useless to line managers, but they also often yield flawed results.

The best companies have tended to focus on customer retention rates, but that measurement is merely the best of a mediocre lot. Retention rates provide, in many industries, a valuable link to profitability, but their relationship to growth is tenuous. That's because they basically track customer defections—the degree to which a bucket is emptying rather filling up. Furthermore, as I have noted, retention rates are a poor indication of customer loyalty in situations where customers are held hostage by high switching costs or other barriers, or where customers naturally outgrow a product because of their aging, increased income, or other factors. You'd want a stronger connection between retention and growth before you went ahead and invested significant money based only on data about retention.

An even less reliable means of gauging loyalty is through conventional customer-satisfaction measures. Our research indicates that satisfaction lacks a consistently demonstrable connection to actual customer behavior and growth. This finding is borne out by the short shrift that investors give to such reports as the American Consumer Satisfaction Index. The ACSI, published quarterly in the *Wall Street Journal,* reflects the customer satisfaction ratings of some 200 U.S. companies. In general, it is difficult to discern a strong correlation between high customer satisfaction scores and outstanding sales growth. Indeed, in some cases, there is an inverse relationship; at Kmart, for example, a significant increase in the company's ACSI rating was accompanied by a sharp decrease in sales as it slid into bankruptcy.

Even the most sophisticated satisfaction measurement systems have serious flaws. I saw this firsthand at one of the Big Three car manufacturers. The marketing executive at the company wanted to understand why, after the firm had spent millions of dollars on customer satisfaction surveys, satisfaction ratings for individual dealers did not relate very closely to dealer profits or growth. When I interviewed dealers, they agreed that customer satisfaction seemed like a reasonable goal. But they also pointed out that other factors were far more important to their profits and growth, such as keeping pressure on salespeople to close a high percentage of leads, filling showrooms with prospects through aggressive advertising, and charging customers the highest possible price for a car.

In most cases, dealers told me, the satisfaction survey is a charade that they play along with to remain in the good graces of the manufacturer and to ensure generous allocations of the hottest-selling models. The pressure they put on salespeople to boost scores often results in postsale pleading with customers to provide top ratings—even if they must offer something like free floor mats or oil changes in return. Dealers are usually complicit with salespeople in this process, a circumstance that further degrades the integrity of these scores. Indeed, some savvy customers negotiate a low price—and then offer to sell the dealer a set of top satisfaction survey ratings for another $500 off the price.

Figuring out a way to accurately measure customer loyalty and satisfaction is extremely important. Companies won't realize the fruits of loyalty until usable measurement systems enable firms to measure their performance against clear loyalty goals—just as they now do in the case of profitability and quality goals. For a while, it seemed as though information technology would provide a means to accurately measure loyalty. Sophisticated customer-relationship-management systems promised to help firms track customer behavior in real time. But the successes thus far have been limited to select industries, such as credit cards or grocery stores, where purchases are so frequent that changes in customer loyalty can be quickly spotted and acted on.

Getting the Facts

So what would be a useful metric for gauging customer loyalty? To find out, I needed to do something rarely undertaken with customer surveys: Match survey responses from individual customers to their actual behavior—repeat purchases and referral patterns—over time. I sought the assistance of Satmetrix, a company that develops software to gather and analyze real-time customer feedback—and on whose board of directors I serve. Teams from Bain also helped with the project.

We started with the roughly 20 questions on the Loyalty Acid Test, a survey that I designed four years ago with Bain colleagues, which does a pretty good job of establishing the state of relations between a company and its customers. (The complete test can be found at http://www.loyaltyrules.com/loyaltyrules/acid_test_cu stomer.html.) We administered the test to thousands of customers recruited from public lists in six industries:

financial services, cable and telephony, personal computers, e-commerce, auto insurance, and Internet service providers.

We then obtained a purchase history for each person surveyed and asked those people to name specific instances in which they had referred someone else to the company in question. When this information wasn't immediately available, we waited six to 12 months and gathered information on subsequent purchases and referrals from those individuals. With information from more than 4,000 customers, we were able to build 14 case studies—that is, cases in which we had sufficient sample sizes to measure the link between survey responses of individual customers of a company and those individuals' actual referral and purchase behavior.

The data allowed us to determine which survey questions had the strongest statistical correlation with repeat purchases or referrals. We hoped that we would find at least one question for each industry that effectively predicted such behaviors, which can drive growth. We found something more: One question was best for *most* industries. "How likely is it that you would recommend [company X] to a friend or colleague?" ranked first or second in 11 of the 14 cases studies. And in two of the three other cases, "would recommend" ranked so close behind the top two predictors that the surveys would be nearly as accurate by relying on results of this single question. (For a ranking of the best-scoring questions, see the sidebar "Ask the Right Question.")

These findings surprised me. My personal bet for the top question (probably reflecting the focus of my

Ask the Right Question

AS PART OF OUR RESEARCH into customer loyalty and growth, my colleagues and I looked for a correlation between survey responses and actual behavior—repeat purchases, or recommendations to friends and peers—that would ultimately lead to profitable growth. Based on information from 4,000 consumers, we ranked a variety of survey questions according to their ability to predict this desirable behavior. (Interestingly, creating a weighted index—based on the responses to multiple questions and taking into account the relative effectiveness of those questions—provided insignificant predictive advantage.)

The top-ranking question was far and away the most effective across industries:

- How likely is it that you would recommend [company X] to a friend or colleague?

Two questions were effective predictors in certain industries:

- How strongly do you agree that [company X] deserves your loyalty?
- How likely is it that you will continue to purchase products/services from [company X]?

Other questions, while useful in a particular industry, had little general applicability:

- How strongly do you agree that [company X] sets the standard for excellence in its industry?
- How strongly do you agree that [company X] makes it easy for you to do business with it?
- If you were selecting a similar provider for the first time, how likely is it that you would you choose [company X]?
- How strongly do you agree that [company X] creates innovative solutions that make your life easier?
- How satisfied are you with [company X's] overall performance?

research on employee loyalty in recent years) would have been "How strongly do you agree that [company X] deserves your loyalty?" Clearly, though, the abstract concept of loyalty was less compelling to customers than what may be the ultimate act of loyalty, a recommendation to a friend. I also expected that "How strongly do you agree that [company X] sets the standard for excellence in its industry?"—with its implications of offering customers both economic benefit and fair treatment—would prove more predictive than it did. One result did not startle me at all. The question "How satisfied are you with [company X's] overall performance?" while relevant in certain industries, would prove to be a relatively weak predictor of growth.

So my colleagues and I had the right question—"How likely is it that you would recommend [company X] to a friend or colleague?"—and now we needed to develop a scale to score the responses. This may seem somewhat trivial, but, as statisticians know, it's not. Making customer loyalty a strategic goal that managers can work toward requires a scale as simple and unambiguous as the question itself. The right one will effectively divide customers into practical groups deserving different attention and organizational responses. It must be intuitive to customers when they assign grades and to employees and partners responsible for interpreting the results and taking action. Ideally, the scale would be so easy to understand that even outsiders, such as investors, regulators, and journalists, would grasp the basic messages without needing a handbook and a statistical abstract.

For these reasons, we settled on a scale where ten means "extremely likely" to recommend, five means neutral, and zero means "not at all likely." When we examined customer referral and repurchase behaviors along this scale, we found three logical clusters. "Promoters," the customers with the highest rates of repurchase and referral, gave ratings of nine or ten to the question. The "passively satisfied" logged a seven or an eight, and "detractors" scored from zero to six.

By limiting the promoter designation to only the most enthusiastic customers, we avoided the "grade inflation" that often infects traditional customer-satisfaction assessments, in which someone a molecule north of neutral is considered "satisfied." (This was the danger that Enterprise Rent-A-Car avoided when it decided to focus on its most enthusiastic customers.) And not only did clustering customers into three categories—promoters, the passively satisfied, and detractors—turn out to provide the simplest, most intuitive, and best predictor of customer behavior; it also made sense to frontline managers, who could relate to the goal of increasing the number of promoters and reducing the number of detractors more readily than increasing the mean of their satisfaction index by one standard deviation.

The Growth Connection

All of our analysis to this point had focused on customer survey responses and how well those linked to customers' referral and repurchase behavior at 14 companies in six industries. But the real test would be how well this approach explained relative growth rates for all competitors in an industry—and across a broader range of industry sectors.

In the first quarter of 2001, Satmetrix began tracking the "would recommend" scores of a new universe of customers, many thousands of them from more than 400 companies in more than a dozen industries. In each subsequent quarter, they then gathered 10,000 to 15,000 responses to a very brief e-mail survey that asked respondents (drawn again from public sources, not Satmetrix's internal client customer lists) to rate one or two companies with which they were familiar. Where we could obtain comparable and reliable revenue-growth data for a range of competitors, and where there were sufficient consumer responses, we plotted each firm's net promoters—the percentage of promoters minus the percentage of detractors—against the company's revenue growth rate.

The results were striking. In airlines, for example, a strong correlation existed between net-promoter figures and a company's average growth rate over the three-year period from 1999 to 2002. Remarkably, this one simple statistic seemed to explain the relative growth rates across the entire industry; that is, no airline has found a way to increase growth without improving its ratio of promoters to detractors. That result was reflected, to a greater or lesser degree, in most of the industries we examined—including rental cars, where Enterprise enjoys both the highest rate of growth and the highest net-promoter percentage among its competitors. (See the exhibit "Growth by Word of Mouth.")

Growth by word of mouth

Research shows that, in most industries, there is a strong correlation between a company's growth rate and the percentage of its customers who are "promoters"—that is, those who say they are extremely likely to recommend the company to a friend or colleague. (The net-promoter figure is calculated by subtracting the percentage of customers who say they are unlikely to make a recommendation from the percentage who say they are extremely likely to do so.) It's worth noting that the size of companies has no relationship to their net-promoter status.

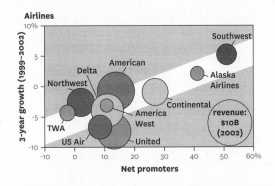

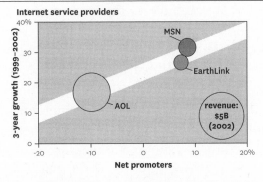

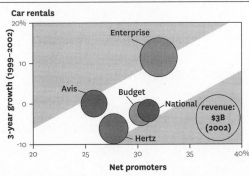

The "would recommend" question wasn't the best predictor of growth in every case. In a few situations, it was simply irrelevant. In database software or computer systems, for instance, senior executives select vendors, and top managers typically didn't appear on the public e-mail lists we used to sample customers. Asking users of the system whether they would recommend the system to a friend or colleague seemed a little abstract, as they had no choice in the matter. In these cases, we found that the "sets the standard of excellence" or "deserves your loyalty" questions were more predictive.

Not surprisingly, "would recommend" also didn't predict relative growth in industries dominated by monopolies and near monopolies, where consumers have little choice. For example, in the local telephone and cable TV businesses, population growth and economic expansion in the region determine growth rates, not how well customers are treated by their suppliers. And in certain cases, we found small niche companies that were growing faster than their net-promoter percentages would imply. But for most companies in most industries, getting customers enthusiastic enough to recommend a company appears to be crucial to growth. (To calculate your own net-promoter number, see the sidebar "A Net-Promoter Primer.")

The Dangers of Detractors

The battle for growth among Internet service providers AOL, MSN, and EarthLink brings to life our findings. For years, market leader AOL aggressively focused on new customer acquisition. Through those efforts, AOL more than offset a substantial number of defections. But the company paid much less attention to converting these new customers into intensely loyal promoters. Customer service lapsed, to the point where customers couldn't even find a phone number to contact company representatives to answer questions or resolve problems.

Today, AOL is struggling to grow. Even though AOL's customer count surged to an eventual peak of 35 million, its deteriorating mix of promoters and detractors eventually choked off expansion. The fire hose of new customer flow—filled with people attracted to free trial promotions—couldn't keep up with the leaks in AOL's customer bucket. Defection rates exceeded 200,000 customers per month in 2003. Marketing costs were ratcheted up to stem the tide, and those expenditures, along with the collapse of online advertising, contributed to declines in cash flow of almost 40% between 2001 and 2003.

By 2002, our research found, 42% of the company's customers were detractors, while only 32% were promoters, giving the company a net-promoter percentage of −10%. The current management team is working on the problem, but it's a challenging one because disappointed customers are undoubtedly spreading their opinions about AOL to family, friends, colleagues, and acquaintances.

AOL's dial-up competitors have done a better job in building promoters, and it shows in their relative rates of growth. MSN invested $500 million in R&D to

A Net-Promoter Primer

TRACKING NET PROMOTERS—the percentage of customers who are promoters of a brand or company minus the percentage who are detractors—offers organizations a powerful way to measure and manage customer loyalty. Firms with the highest net-promoter scores consistently garner the lion's share of industry growth. So how can companies get started?

Survey a statistically valid sample of your customers with the following question: "How likely is it that you would recommend [brand or company X] to a friend or colleague?" It's critical to provide a consistent scale for responses that range from zero to ten, where zero means not at all likely, five means neutral, and ten means extremely likely.

Resist the urge to let survey questions multiply; more questions diminish response rates along with the reliability of your sample. You need only one question to determine the status—promoter, passively satisfied, or detractor—of a customer. (Follow-up questions can help unearth the reasons for customers' feelings and point to profitable remedies. But such questions should be tailored to the three categories of customers. Learning how to turn a passively satisfied customer into a promoter requires a very different line of questioning from learning how to resolve the problems of a detractor.)

upgrade its service with functional improvements such as improved parental controls and spam filters. By 2003, MSN's promoter population reached 41% of its customer base, compared with a detractor population of 32%, giving the company a net-promoter percentage of 9%. EarthLink managed to nearly match MSN's net-promoter score over this period by continuing to invest in the reliability of its dial-up connections (minimizing

Calculate the percentage of customers who respond with nine or ten (promoters) and the percentage who respond with zero through six (detractors). Subtract the percentage of detractors from the percentage of promoters to arrive at your net-promoter score. Don't be surprised if your score is lower than you expect. The median net-promoter score of more than 400 companies in 28 industries (based on some 130,000 customer survey responses gathered over the past two-plus years by Satmetrix, a maker of software for managing real-time customer feedback) was just 16%.

Compare net-promoter scores from specific regions, branches, service or sales reps, and customer segments. This often reveals root causes of differences as well as best practices that can be shared. What really counts, of course, is how your company compares with direct competitors. Have your market researchers survey your competitors' customers using the same method. You can then determine how your company stacks up within your industry and whether your current net-promoter number is a competitive asset or a liability.

Improve your score. The companies with the most enthusiastic customer referrals, including eBay, Amazon, and USAA, receive net-promoter scores of 75% to more than 80%. For companies aiming to garner world-class loyalty—and the growth that comes with it—this should be the target.

the irritation of busy signals and dropped connections) and by making phone support readily available.

AOL's experience vividly illustrates the folly of seeking growth through shortcuts such as massive price cuts or other incentives rather than through building true loyalty. It also illustrates the detrimental effect that detractors' word-of-mouth communications can have on a business—the flip side of customers' recommendations to their friends. Countering a damaged reputation requires a company to create tremendously appealing incentives that will persuade skeptical customers to give a product or service a try, and the incentives drive up already significant customer acquisition costs.

Furthermore, detractors—and even customers who are only passively satisfied but not enthusiastically loyal—typically take a toll on employees and increase service costs. Finally, every detractor represents a missed opportunity to add a promoter to the customer population, one more unpaid salesperson to market your product or service and generate growth.

Keep It Simple

One of the main takeaways from our research is that companies can keep customer surveys simple. The most basic surveys—employing the right questions— can allow companies to report timely data that are easy to act on. Too many of today's satisfaction survey processes yield complex information that's months out of date by the time it reaches frontline managers. Good luck to the branch manager who tries to help an employee interpret a score resulting from a complex weighting algorithm based on feedback from anonymous customers, many of whom were surveyed before the employee had his current job.

Contrast that scenario with one in which a manager presents employees with numbers from the previous week (or day) showing the percentages (and names) of a branch office's customers who are promoters, passively satisfied, and detractors—and then issues the managerial charge, "We need more promoters and fewer detractors in order to grow." The goal is clear-cut, actionable, and motivating.

In short, a customer feedback program should be viewed not as "market research" but as an operating management tool. Again, consider Enterprise Rent-A-Car. The first step in the development of Enterprise's current system was to devise a way to track loyalty by measuring service quality from the customer's perspective. The initial effort yielded a long, unwieldy research questionnaire, one that included the pet questions of everyone involved in drafting the survey. It only captured average service quality on a regional basis—interesting, but useless, since managers needed to see scores for each individual branch to establish clear accountability. Over time, the sample was expanded to provide this information. And the number of questions on the survey was sharply reduced; this simplified the collating of answers and allowed the company to post monthly branch-level results almost as soon as they were collected.

The company then began examining the relationships between customer responses and actual purchases and referrals. This is when Enterprise learned the value of enthusiasts. Customers who gave the highest rating to their rental experience were three times more likely to rent again than those who gave Enterprise the second-highest grade. When a customer reported a neutral or negative experience, marking him a potential detractor, the interviewer requested permission to immediately forward this information to the branch manager, who was trained how to apologize, identify the root cause of the problem, and resolve it.

The measurement system cost more than $4 million per year, but the company made such significant progress in building customer loyalty that the company's management considers it one of the company's best investments. And the new system had definitely started to get employees' attention. In fact, a few branch managers (perhaps taking a cue from car dealers) attempted to manipulate the system to their benefit. Enterprise responded with a process for spotting—for example, by ensuring that the phone numbers of dissatisfied respondents hadn't been changed, making it difficult to follow up—and punishing "gamers."

Despite the system's success, CEO Andy Taylor felt something was missing. Branch scores were not improving quickly enough, and a big gap continued to separate the worst- and best-performing regions. Taylor's assessment: "We needed a greater sense of urgency." So the management team decided that field managers would not be eligible for promotion unless their branch or group of branches matched or exceeded the company's average scores. That's a pretty radical idea when you think about it: giving customers, in effect, veto power over managerial pay raises and promotions.

The rigorous implementation of this simple customer feedback system had a clear impact on business. As the survey scores rose, so did Enterprise's growth relative to its competition. Taylor cites the linking of customer feedback to employee rewards as one of the most important reasons that Enterprise has continued to grow, even as the business became bigger and, arguably, more mature. (For more on Enterprise's customer survey program, see "Driving Customer Satisfaction," HBR July 2002.)

Converting Customers into Promoters

If collecting and applying customer feedback is this simple, why don't companies already do it this way? I don't want to be too cynical, but perhaps the research firms that administer current customer surveys know there is very little profit margin for them in something as bare-bones as this. Complex loyalty indexes, based on a dozen or more proprietary questions and weighted with a black-box scaling function, simply generate more business for survey firms.

The market research firms have an even deeper fear. With the advent of e-mail and analytical software, leading-edge companies can now bypass the research firms entirely, cutting costs and improving the quality and timeliness of feedback. These new tools enable companies to gather customer feedback and report results in real time, funneling it directly to frontline employees and managers. This can also threaten in-house market research departments, which typically have built their power base through controlling and interpreting customer survey data. Marketing departments understandably focus surveys on the areas they can control, such as brand image, pricing, and product features. But a customer's willingness to recommend to a friend results from how well the customer is treated by frontline employees, which in turn is determined by all the functional areas that contribute to a customer's experience.

For a measure to be practical, operational, and reliable—that is, for it to determine the percentage of net promoters among customers and allow managers to act on it—the process and the results need to be owned and accepted by all of the business functions. And all the people in the organization must know which customers they are responsible for. Overseeing such a process is a more appropriate task for the CFO, or for the general manager of the business unit, than for the marketing department. Indeed, it is too important (and politically charged) to delegate to any one function.

The path to sustainable, profitable growth begins with creating more promoters and fewer detractors and making your net-promoter number transparent throughout your organization. This number is the one number you need to grow. It's that simple and that profound.

FREDERICK F. REICHHELD is a director emeritus of the consulting firm Bain & Company and a Bain Fellow.

Originally published in December 2003. Reprint R0312C

Putting the Service-Profit Chain to Work

by James L. Heskett, Thomas O. Jones, Gary W. Loveman, W. Earl Sasser, Jr., and Leonard A. Schlesinger

TOP-LEVEL EXECUTIVES OF outstanding service organizations spend little time setting profit goals or focusing on market share, the management mantra of the 1970s and 1980s. Instead, they understand that in the new economics of service, frontline workers and customers need to be the center of management concern. Successful service managers pay attention to the factors that drive profitability in this new service paradigm: investment in people, technology that supports frontline workers, revamped recruiting and training practices, and compensation linked to performance for employees at every level. And they express a vision of leadership in terms rarely heard in corporate America: an organization's "patina of spirituality," the "importance of the mundane."

A growing number of companies that includes Banc One, Intuit, Southwest Airlines, ServiceMaster, USAA, Taco Bell, and MCI know that when they make employees and customers paramount, a radical shift occurs in the way they manage and measure success. The new economics of service requires innovative measurement techniques. These techniques calibrate the impact of employee satisfaction, loyalty, and productivity on the value of products and services delivered so that managers can build customer satisfaction and loyalty and assess the corresponding impact on profitability and growth. In fact, the lifetime value of a loyal customer can be astronomical, especially when referrals are added to the economics of customer retention and repeat purchases of related products. For example, the lifetime revenue stream from a loyal pizza eater can be $8,000, a Cadillac owner $332,000, and a corporate purchaser of commercial aircraft literally billions of dollars.

The service-profit chain, developed from analyses of successful service organizations, puts "hard" values on "soft" measures. It helps managers target new investments to develop service and satisfaction levels for maximum competitive impact, widening the gap between service leaders and their merely good competitors.

The Service-Profit Chain

The service-profit chain establishes relationships between profitability, customer loyalty, and employee satisfaction, loyalty, and productivity. The links in the

Idea in Brief

What drives growth and profitability in a service business? Highly satisfied customers. And to keep those customers profitable, you need to manage *all* the aspects of your operation that affect customer satisfaction—what the authors call the **service-profit chain**.

Here's how the service-profit chain works: Employee satisfaction soars when you enhance *internal service quality* (equipping employees with the skills and power to serve customers). Employee satisfaction in turn fuels *employee loyalty*, which raises *employee productivity*. Higher productivity means greater *external service value*

for customers—which enhances *customer satisfaction* and *loyalty*. A mere 5% jump in customer loyalty can boost profits 25% to 85%.

To maximize your profits, strengthen all the links in your service-profit chain. For example, fast-food giant Taco Bell found that its stores with low workforce turnover (a key marker of employee loyalty) enjoyed double the sales and 55% higher profits than stores with high turnover. To boost profitability across stores, it enhanced internal service quality—for instance, by giving employees more latitude for on-the-job decision making.

chain (which should be regarded as propositions) are as follows: Profit and growth are stimulated primarily by customer loyalty. Loyalty is a direct result of customer satisfaction. Satisfaction is largely influenced by the value of services provided to customers. Value is created by satisfied, loyal, and productive employees. Employee satisfaction, in turn, results primarily from high-quality support services and policies that enable employees to deliver results to customers. (See the exhibit "The Links in the Service-Profit Chain.")

The service-profit chain is also defined by a special kind of leadership. CEOs of exemplary service companies emphasize the importance of each employee and

Idea in Practice

To optimize your profitability, the authors recommend these practices.

Understand the Links in the Service-Profit Chain

Starting with internal service quality, each link in the service-profit chain can directly strengthen—or weaken—the next:

This link . . .	. . . affects this link	Example
Internal service quality	Employee satisfaction	Financial-services company USAA makes it easier for call-center reps to achieve results for customers by equipping them with state-of-the-art information systems. It also offers more than 200 courses in its employee development program.
Employee satisfaction	Employee loyalty	At Southwest Airlines, employee satisfaction levels are so high that at some of its operating locations, turnover rates are lower than 5% per year.
Employee loyalty	Employee productivity	An experienced broker who stays with a securities firm for five or more years may account for $2+ million in revenue over several years.
Employee productivity	External service value	Thanks to Southwest employees' unusual productivity (including rapid deplaning and reloading), customer perceptions of service value are very high—even though Southwest doesn't assign seats or offer meals.
External service value	Customer satisfaction	Insurance provider Progressive creates service value for customers by sending teams to the scene of major accidents and providing support services like transportation and housing. By processing and paying claims quickly and reducing policyholder effort, the company enhances customer satisfaction.

This link . . .	. . . affects this link	Example
Customer satisfaction	Customer loyalty	Xerox found that customers who rated their satisfaction level with the company with a "5" ("very satisfied") on a scale of 1 to 5 were six times as likely to demonstrate loyalty—by repurchasing Xerox equipment—as those who rated their satisfaction level with a "4" ("satisfied").
Customer loyalty	Growth and profitability	By regularly taking steps to improve customer loyalty, Banc One achieved a return on assets more than double that of its competitors.

Measure—and Manage—the Relationships in Your Service-Profit Chain

To enhance profitability, measure the relationships between links in your company's service-profit chain. Then fashion strategies for strengthening them.

Example: To assess the relationship between **internal service quality** and **employee satisfaction,** Taco Bell: 1) Monitors **internal service quality** through a network of 800 numbers created to answer employees' questions, field their complaints, remedy situations, and alert top-level management to potential trouble spots. 2) Conducts periodic employee roundtable meetings, interviews, and companywide surveys to measure **employee satisfaction**. The results of this work prompted Taco Bell to design an employee satisfaction program that features a new selection process, improved skill building, and automation of unpleasant "back room" labor.

The links in the service-profit chain

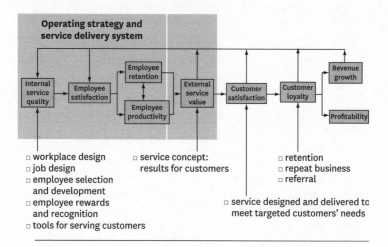

- □ workplace design
- □ job design
- □ employee selection and development
- □ employee rewards and recognition
- □ tools for serving customers

- □ service concept: results for customers

- □ service designed and delivered to meet targeted customers' needs

- □ retention
- □ repeat business
- □ referral

customer. For these CEOs, the focus on customers and employees is no empty slogan tailored to an annual management meeting. For example, Herbert Kelleher, CEO of Southwest Airlines, can be found aboard airplanes, on tarmacs, and in terminals, interacting with employees and customers. Kelleher believes that hiring employees who have the right attitude is so important that the hiring process takes on a "patina of spirituality." In addition, he believes that "anyone who looks at things solely in terms of factors that can easily be quantified is missing the heart of business, which is people." William Pollard, the chairman of Service-Master, continually underscores the importance of "teacher-learner" managers, who have what he calls "a servant's heart." And John McCoy, CEO of Banc One, stresses the "uncommon partnership," a system of support that provides maximum latitude to individual bank presidents while supplying information systems and common measurements of customer satisfaction and financial measures.

A closer look at each link reveals how the service-profit chain functions as a whole.

Customer Loyalty Drives Profitability and Growth

To maximize profit, managers have pursued the Holy Grail of becoming number one or two in their industries for nearly two decades. Recently, however, new measures of service industries like software and banking suggest that customer loyalty is a more important determinant of profit. (See Frederick F. Reichheld and W. Earl Sasser, Jr., "Zero Defections: Quality Comes to Services," HBR September–October 1990.) Reichheld and Sasser estimate that a 5% increase in customer loyalty can produce profit increases from 25% to 85%. They conclude that *quality* of market share, measured in terms of customer loyalty, deserves as much attention as *quantity* of share.

Banc One, based in Columbus, Ohio, has developed a sophisticated system to track several factors involved in customer loyalty and satisfaction. Once driven strictly by financial measures, Banc One now conducts quarterly measures of customer retention; the number of services used by each customer, or *depth of relationship*; and the level of customer satisfaction. The strategies derived from this information help explain why Banc One has achieved a return on assets more than double that of its competitors in recent years.

Customer Satisfaction Drives Customer Loyalty

Leading service companies are currently trying to quantify customer satisfaction. For example, for several years, Xerox has polled 480,000 customers per year regarding product and service satisfaction using a five-point scale from 5 (high) to 1 (low). Until two years ago, Xerox's goal was to achieve 100% 4s (satisfied) and 5s (very satisfied) by the end of 1993. But in 1991, an analysis of customers who gave Xerox 4s and 5s on satisfaction found that the relationships between the scores and actual loyalty differed greatly depending on whether the customers were very satisfied or satisfied. Customers giving Xerox 5s were six times more likely to repurchase Xerox equipment than those giving 4s.

This analysis led Xerox to extend its efforts to create *apostles*—a term coined by Scott D. Cook, CEO of software producer and distributor Intuit, describing customers so satisfied that they convert the uninitiated to a product or service. Xerox's management currently wants to achieve 100% apostles, or 5s, by the end of 1996 by upgrading service levels and guaranteeing customer satisfaction. But just as important for Xerox's profitability is to avoid creating *terrorists*: customers so unhappy that they speak out against a poorly delivered service at every opportunity. Terrorists can reach hundreds of potential customers. In some instances, they

A satisfied customer is loyal

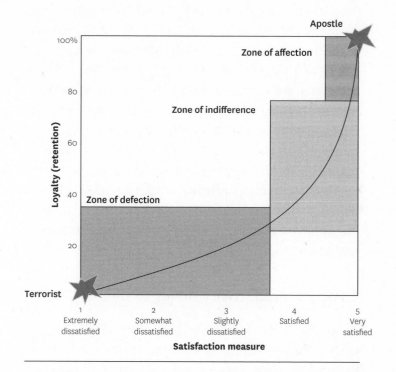

can even discourage acquaintances from trying a service or product. (See the exhibit "A Satisfied Customer Is Loyal.")

Value Drives Customer Satisfaction

Customers today are strongly value oriented. But just what does that mean? Customers tell us that value means the results they receive in relation to the total costs (both the price and other costs to customers incurred in acquiring the service). The insurance company Progressive is creating just this kind of value for its customers by processing and paying claims quickly and with little policyholder effort. Members of the company's CAT (catastrophe) team fly to the scene of major accidents, providing support services like transportation and housing and handling claims rapidly. By reducing legal costs and actually placing more money in the hands of the injured parties, the CAT team more than makes up for the added expenses the organization incurs by maintaining the team. In addition, the CAT team delivers value to customers, which helps explain why Progressive has one of the highest margins in the property-and-casualty insurance industry.

Employee Productivity Drives Value

At Southwest Airlines, the seventh-largest U.S. domestic carrier, an astonishing story of employee productivity occurs daily. Eighty-six percent of the company's 14,000 employees are unionized. Positions are designed so that employees can perform several jobs if necessary. Schedules, routes, and company practices—such as open seating and the use of simple, color-coded, reusable boarding passes—enable the boarding of three and four times more passengers per day than competing airlines. In fact, Southwest deplanes and reloads two-thirds of its flights in 15 minutes or less. Because of aircraft availability and short-haul routes that don't require long layovers for flight crews, Southwest has roughly 40% more pilot and aircraft utilization than its major competitors: Its pilots fly on average 70 hours per month versus 50 hours at other airlines. These factors explain how the company can charge fares from 60% to 70% lower than existing fares in markets it enters.

At Southwest, customer perceptions of value are very high, even though the airline does not assign seats, offer meals, or integrate its reservation system with other airlines. Customers place high value on Southwest's frequent departures, on-time service, friendly employees, and very low fares. Southwest's management knows this because its major marketing research unit—its 14,000 employees—is in daily contact with customers and reports its findings back to management. In addition, the Federal Aviation Administration's performance measures show that Southwest, of all the major airlines, regularly achieves the highest level of on-time arrivals, the lowest number of complaints, and the fewest lost-baggage claims per 1,000 passengers. When combined with Southwest's low fares per seat-mile, these indicators show the higher value delivered by Southwest's employees compared with most domestic competitors. Southwest has been profitable for 21 consecutive years and was the only major airline to realize a profit in 1992. (See the exhibit "How Southwest Compares with Its Competitors.")

Employee Loyalty Drives Productivity

Traditional measures of the losses incurred by employee turnover concentrate only on the cost of recruiting,

How Southwest compares with its competitors

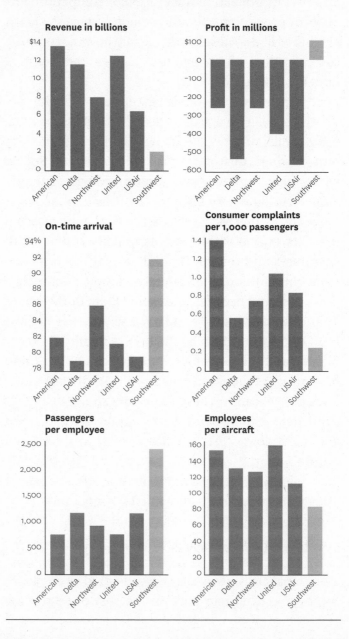

Revenue in billions

Profit in millions

On-time arrival

Consumer complaints per 1,000 passengers

Passengers per employee

Employees per aircraft

hiring, and training replacements. In most service jobs, the real cost of turnover is the loss of productivity and decreased customer satisfaction. One recent study of an automobile dealer's sales personnel by Abt Associates concluded that the average monthly cost of replacing a sales representative who had five to eight years of experience with an employee who had less than one year of experience was as much as $36,000 in sales. And the costs of losing a valued broker at a securities firm can be still more dire. Conservatively estimated, it takes nearly five years for a broker to rebuild relationships with customers that can return $1 million per year in commissions to the brokerage house—a cumulative loss of at least $2.5 million in commissions.

Employee Satisfaction Drives Loyalty

In one 1991 proprietary study of a property-and-casualty insurance company's employees, 30% of all dissatisfied employees registered an intention to leave the company, a potential turnover rate three times higher than that for satisfied employees. In this same case, low employee turnover was found to be linked closely to high customer satisfaction. In contrast, Southwest Airlines, recently named one of the country's 10 best places to work, experiences the highest rate of employee retention in the airline industry. Satisfaction levels are so high that at some of its operating locations, employee turnover rates are less than 5% per year. USAA, a major provider of insurance and other financial services by direct mail and phone, also achieves low levels of employee turnover by ensuring that its employees are highly satisfied. But what drives employee satisfaction? Is it compensation, perks, or plush workplaces?

Internal Quality Drives Employee Satisfaction

What we call the *internal quality* of a working environment contributes most to employee satisfaction. Internal quality is measured by the feelings that employees have toward their jobs, colleagues, and companies. What do service employees value most on the job? Although our data are preliminary at best, they point increasingly to the ability and authority of service workers to achieve results for customers. At USAA, for example, telephone sales and service representatives are backed by a sophisticated information system that puts complete customer information files at their fingertips the instant they receive a customer's call. In addition, state-of-the-art, job-related training is made available to USAA employees. And the curriculum goes still further, with 200 courses in 75 classrooms on a wide range of subjects.

Internal quality is also characterized by the attitudes that people have toward one another and the way people serve each other inside the organization. For example, ServiceMaster, a provider of a range of cleaning and maintenance services, aims to maximize the dignity of the individual service worker. Each year, it analyzes in depth a part of the maintenance process, such as cleaning a floor, in order to reduce the time and effort needed to complete the task. The "importance of the mundane" is stressed repeatedly in ServiceMaster's management training—for example, in the seven-step process devised for cleaning a hospital room: from the first step, greeting the patient, to the last step, asking patients whether or not they need anything else done. Using this process, service workers develop communication skills and learn to interact with patients in ways that add depth and dimension to their jobs.

Leadership Underlies the Chain's Success

Leaders who understand the service-profit chain develop and maintain a corporate culture centered on service to customers and fellow employees. They display a willingness and ability to listen. Successful CEOs like John Martin of Taco Bell, John McCoy of Banc One, Herb Kelleher of Southwest, and Bill Pollard of Service-Master spend a great deal of time with customers and employees, experiencing their companies' service processes while listening to employees for suggestions for improvement. They care about their employees and spend a great deal of time selecting, tracking, and recognizing them.

For example, Brigadier General Robert McDermott, until recently chairman and CEO of USAA, reflected, "Public recognition of outstanding employees flows naturally from our corporate culture. That culture is talked about all the time, and we live it." According to Scott Cook at Intuit, "Most people take culture as a given. It is around you, the thinking goes, and you can't do anything about it. However, when you run a company, you have the opportunity to determine the culture. I find that when you champion the most noble values—including service, analysis, and database decision making—employees rise to the challenge, and you forever change their lives."

Relating Links in the Chain for Management Action

While many organizations are beginning to measure relationships between individual links in the service-profit chain, only a few have related the links in meaningful ways—ways that can lead to comprehensive strategies for achieving lasting competitive advantage.

The 1991 proprietary study of a property-and-casualty insurance company, cited earlier, not only identified the links between employee satisfaction and loyalty but also established that a primary source of job satisfaction was the service workers' perceptions of their ability to meet customer needs. Those who felt they did meet customer needs registered job satisfaction levels more than twice as high as those who felt they didn't. But even more important, the same study found that when a service worker left the company, customer satisfaction levels dropped sharply, from 75% to 55%. As a result of this analysis, management is trying to reduce turnover among customer-contact employees and to enhance their job skills.

Similarly, in a study of its seven telephone customer service centers, MCI found clear relationships between employees' perceptions of the quality of MCI service and employee satisfaction. The study also linked employee satisfaction directly to customer satisfaction and intentions to continue to use MCI services. Identifying these relationships motivated MCI's management to probe deeper and determine what affected job satisfaction at the service centers. The factors they uncovered, in order of importance, were satisfaction with the job itself, training, pay, advancement fairness, treatment with respect and dignity, teamwork, and the company's interest in employees' well-being. Armed with this information, MCI's management began examining its policies concerning those items valued most by employees at its service centers. MCI has incorporated information about its service capabilities into training and communications efforts and television advertising.

No organization has made a more comprehensive effort to measure relationships in the service-profit chain and fashion a strategy around them than the fast-food company Taco Bell, a subsidiary of PepsiCo. Taco Bell's management tracks profits daily by unit, market manager, zone, and country. By integrating this information with the results of exit interviews that Taco Bell conducts with 800,000 customers annually, management has found that stores in the top quadrant of customer satisfaction ratings outperform the others by all measures. As a result, it has linked no less than 20% of all operations managers' compensation in company-owned stores to customer satisfaction ratings, realizing a subsequent increase in both customer satisfaction ratings and profits.

However, Taco Bell's efforts don't stop there. By examining employee turnover records for individual stores, Taco Bell has discovered that the 20% of stores with the lowest turnover rates enjoy double the sales and 55% higher profits than the 20% of stores with the highest employee turnover rates. As a result of this self-examination, Taco Bell has instituted financial and other incentives in order to reverse the cycle of failure that is associated with poor employee selection, subpar training, low pay, and high turnover.

In addition, Taco Bell monitors internal quality through a network of 800 numbers created to answer employees' questions, field their complaints, remedy situations, and alert top-level management to potential trouble spots. It also conducts periodic employee roundtable meetings, interviews, and a comprehensive companywide survey every two or three years in order to measure satisfaction. As a result of all this work, Taco Bell's employee satisfaction program features a new selection process, improved skill building, increased latitude for decision making on the job, further automation of unpleasant backroom labor, and, finally, greater opportunities for employee promotion into management positions.

Relating all the links in the service-profit chain may seem to be a tall order. But profitability depends not only on placing hard values on soft measures but also on linking those individual measures together into a comprehensive service picture. Service organizations need to quantify their investments in people—both customers and employees. The service-profit chain provides the framework for this critical task.

Service-Profit Chain Audit

A service-profit chain audit helps companies determine what drives their profit and suggests actions that can lead to long-term profitability. As they review the audit, managers should ask themselves what efforts are under way to obtain answers to the following questions and what those answers reveal about their companies.

Profit and Growth

How do we define loyal customers? Customers often become more profitable over time. And loyal customers account for an unusually high proportion of the sales and profit growth of successful service providers. In some organizations, loyalty is measured in terms of whether or not a customer is on the company rolls. But several companies have found that their most loyal customers—the top 20% of total customers—not only provide all the profit but also cover losses incurred in dealing with less loyal customers.

Because of the link between loyal customers and profit, Banc One measures depth of relationship—the number of available related financial services, such as checking, lending, and safe deposit, actually used by customers. Recognizing the same relationship, Taco Bell measures "share of stomach" to assess the company's sales against all other food purchases a customer can potentially make. As a result, the fast-food chain is trying to reach consumers through kiosks, carts, trucks, and the shelves of supermarkets.

Do measurements of customer profitability include profits from referrals? Companies that measure the stream of revenue and profits from loyal customers (retention) and repeat sales often overlook what can be the most important of the three Rs of loyalty: referrals. For example, Intuit provides high-quality, free lifetime service for a personal finance software package that sells for as little as $30. The strategy makes sense when the value of a loyal customer is considered—a revenue stream of several thousands of dollars from software updates, supplies, and new customer referrals. With this strategy in place, Intuit increased its sales to more than $30 million with just two U.S. field sales representatives.

What proportion of business development expenditures and incentives are directed to the retention of existing customers? Too many companies concentrate nearly all their efforts on attracting new customers. But in businesses like life insurance, a new policyholder doesn't become profitable for at least three years. In the credit-card finance business, the break-even point for a new customer is often six or more years because of high marketing and bad-debt costs in the first year of a relationship with cardholders. These costs must be defrayed by profits from loyal customers, suggesting the need for a careful division of organizational effort between customer retention and development.

Why do our customers defect? It's important to find out not only where defectors go but also why they defect. Was it because of poor service, price, or value? Answers to these questions provide information about whether or not existing strategies are working. In addition, exit interviews of customers can have real sales impact. For example, at one credit-card service organization, a phone call to question cardholders who had stopped using their cards led to the immediate reinstatement of one-third of the defectors.

Customer Satisfaction

Are customer satisfaction data gathered in an objective, consistent, and periodic fashion? Currently, the weakest measurements being used by the companies we have studied concern customer satisfaction. At some companies, high levels of reported customer satisfaction are contradicted by continuing declines in sales and profits. Upon closer observation, we discovered that the service providers were gaming the data, using manipulative methods for collecting customer satisfaction data. In one extreme case, an automobile dealer sent a questionnaire to recent buyers with the highest marks already filled in, requiring owners to alter the marks only if they disagreed. Companies can, however, obtain more objective results using third-party interviews; "mystery shopping" by unidentified, paid observers; or technologies like touch-screen television.

Consistency is at least as important as the actual questions asked of customers. Some of Banc One's operating units formerly conducted their own customer satisfaction surveys. Today the surveys have been centralized, made mandatory, and are administered by mail on a quarterly basis to around 125,000 customers. When combined with periodic measurement, the surveys provide highly relevant trend information that informs the managerial decision-making process. Similarly, Xerox's measures of satisfaction obtained from 10,000 customers per month—a product of an unchanging set of survey questions and very large samples—make possible period-to-period comparisons that are important in measuring and rewarding performance.

Where are the listening posts for obtaining customer feedback in your organization? Listening posts are tools for collecting data from customers and systematically translating those data into information in order to improve service and products. Common examples are letters of complaint. Still more important listening posts are reports from field sales and service personnel or the logs of telephone service representatives. Intuit's content analysis of customer service inquiries fielded by service representatives produced over 50 software improvements and 100 software documentation improvements in a single year. USAA has gone one step further by automating the feedback process to enter data online, enabling its analysis and plans departments to develop corrective actions.

How is information concerning customer satisfaction used to solve customer problems? In order to handle customer problems, service providers must have the latitude to resolve any situation promptly. In addition, information regarding a customer concern must be transmitted to the service provider quickly. Customers and employees must be encouraged to report rather than suppress concerns. For example, one Boston-area Lexus dealer notified its customers, "If you are experiencing a problem with your car or our service department and you can't answer '100% satisfied' when you receive your survey directly from Lexus, please give us the opportunity to correct the problem before you fill out the survey. Lexus takes its customer surveys very seriously."

External Service Value

How do you measure service value? Value is a function not only of costs to the customer but also of the results achieved for the customer. Value is always relative because it is based both on perceptions of the way a service is delivered and on initial customer expectations. Typically, a company measures value using the reasons expressed by customers for high or low satisfaction. Because value varies with individual expectations, efforts to improve value inevitably require service organizations to move all levels of management closer to the customer and give frontline service employees the latitude to customize a standard service to individual needs.

How is information concerning customers' perceptions of value shared with those responsible for designing a product or service? Relaying information concerning customer expectations to those responsible for design often requires the formation of teams of people responsible for sales, operations, and service or product design, as well as the frequent assignment of service designers to tasks requiring field contact with customers. Intuit has created this kind of capability in product development teams. And all Intuit employees, including the CEO, must periodically work on the customer service phones. Similarly, at Southwest Airlines, those responsible for flight scheduling periodically work shifts in the company's terminals to get a feel for the impact of schedules on customer and employee satisfaction.

To what extent are measures taken of differences between customers' perceptions of quality delivered and their expectations before delivery? Ultimately, service quality is a function of the gap between perceptions of the actual service experienced and what a customer expected before receiving that service. Actual service includes both final results and the process through which those results were obtained. Differences between experiences and expectations can be measured in generic dimensions such as the reliability and timeliness of service, the empathy and authority with which the service was delivered, and the extent to which the customer is left with tangible evidence (like a calling card) that the service has been performed.

Do our organization's efforts to improve external service quality emphasize effective recovery from service errors in addition to providing a service right the first time? A popular concept of quality in manufacturing is the importance of "doing things right the first time." But customers of service organizations often allow one mistake.

Some organizations are very good at delivering service as long as nothing goes wrong. Others organize for and thrive on service emergencies. Outstanding service organizations do both by giving frontline employees the latitude to effect recovery. Southwest Airlines maintains a policy of allowing frontline employees to do whatever they feel comfortable doing in order to satisfy customers. Xerox authorizes frontline service employees to replace up to $250,000 worth of equipment if customers are not getting results.

Employee Productivity

How do you measure employee productivity? To what extent do measures of productivity identify changes in the quality as well as the quantity of service produced per unit of input? In many services, the ultimate measure of quality may be customer satisfaction. That measure should be combined with measures of quantity to determine the total output of the service organization. At ServiceMaster, for example, measures of output in the schools and hospitals cleaned under the company's supervision include both numbers of work orders performed per employee hour and the quality of the work done, as determined by periodic inspections performed by ServiceMaster and client personnel. Similarly, Southwest Airlines delivers relatively high levels of productivity in terms of both quality and quantity. In fact, outstanding service competitors are replacing the typical "either/or" trade-off between quality and quantity with an "and/also" imperative.

Employee Loyalty

How do you create employee loyalty? Employee loyalty goes hand in hand with productivity, contradicting the conventional wisdom that successful service providers should be promoted to larger supervisory responsibilities or moved to a similar job in a larger business unit. ServiceMaster and Taco Bell have expanded jobs without promoting good service workers away from their customers. At ServiceMaster, effective single-unit managers are given supervisory responsibilities for custodial, maintenance, or other workers at more than one hospital or school. Taco Bell gives restaurant general managers a "hunting license" to develop new sales sites in the neighborhoods served by their restaurants and rewards them for doing it.

Have we made an effort to determine the right level of employee retention? Rarely is the right level of retention 100%. Dynamic service organizations require a certain level of turnover. However, in calibrating desired turnover levels, it is important to take into account the full cost of the loss of key service providers, including those of lost sales and productivity and added recruiting, selection, and training.

Employee Satisfaction

Is employee satisfaction measured in ways that can be linked to similar measures of customer satisfaction with sufficient frequency and consistency to establish trends for management use? Taco Bell studies employee satisfaction through surveys, frequent interviews, and roundtable meetings. Customer satisfaction is measured by interviews with customers conducted biannually and includes questions about satisfaction with employee friendliness and hustle. Both the employee and the customer satisfaction rankings are comprehensive, store-specific, and conducted frequently. With these data, the company can better understand overall trends and the links between employee and customer satisfaction.

Are employee selection criteria and methods geared to what customers, as well as managers, believe are important? At Southwest Airlines, for example, frequent fliers are regularly invited to participate in the auditioning and selection of cabin attendants. And many take time off from work to join Southwest's employee selection team as it carries out its work. As one customer commented, "Why not do it? It's my airline."

To what extent are measures of customer satisfaction, customer loyalty, or the quality and quantity of service output used in recognizing and rewarding employees? Employee recognition may often involve little more than informing individual employees or employees as a group about service improvements and individual successes. Banc One goes one step further, including customer satisfaction measures for each banking unit in its periodic report of other performance measures, mostly financial, to all units.

Internal Service Quality

Do employees know who their customers are? It is particularly difficult for employees to identify their customers when those customers are internal to the company. These employees often do not know what impact their work has on other departments. Identifying internal customers requires mapping and communicating characteristics of work flow, organizing periodic cross-departmental meetings between "customers" and "servers," and recognizing good internal service performance.

In 1990, USAA organized a PRIDE (Professionalism Results in Dedication to Excellence) team of 100 employees and managers to examine and improve on a function-by-function basis all processes associated with property-and-casualty insurance administration, which included analyzing customer needs and expectations. The PRIDE effort was so successful that it led to a cross-functional review of USAA's service processing. Service processing time has been reduced, as have handoffs of customers from one server to another.

Are employees satisfied with the technological and personal support they receive on the job? The cornerstone of success at Taco Bell is the provision of the latest in information technology, food service equipment, simple work-scheduling techniques, and effective team training. This practice led to the establishment of self-managing teams of service providers. Also, the quality of work life involves selecting the right workers. Winners like to be associated with winners. Better employees tend to refer people they like and people like themselves. Internal service quality can also be thought of as the quality of work life. It is a visible expression of an organization's culture, one influenced in important ways by leadership.

Leadership

To what extent is the company's leadership:

- *energetic, creative versus stately, conservative?*

- *participatory, caring versus removed, elitist?*

- *listening, coaching, and teaching versus supervising and managing?*

- *motivating by mission versus motivating by fear?*

- *leading by means of personally demonstrated values versus institutionalized policies? How much time is spent by the organization's leadership personally developing and maintaining a corporate culture centered on service to customers and fellow employees?*

Leaders naturally have individual traits and styles. But the CEOs of companies that are successfully using the service-profit chain possess all or most of a set of traits that separate them from their merely good competitors. Of course, different styles of leadership are appropriate for various stages in an organization's development. But the messages sent by the successful leaders we have observed stress the importance of careful attention to the needs of customers and employees. These leaders create a culture capable of adapting to the needs of both.

Relating the Measures

What are the most important relationships in your company's service-profit chain? To what extent does each measure correlate with profit and growth at the frontline level? Is the importance of these relationships reflected in rewards and incentives offered to employees? Measures drive action when they are related in ways that provide managers with direction. To enjoy the kind of success that service organizations like Southwest Airlines, ServiceMaster, and Taco Bell have enjoyed, looking at individual measures is not enough. Only if the individual measures are tied together into a comprehensive picture will the service-profit chain provide a foundation for unprecedented profit and growth.

JAMES L. HESKETT is a Baker Foundation Professor, Emeritus, at Harvard Business School. **THOMAS O. JONES** is the president of eLanes, in Andover, Massachusetts. **GARY W. LOVEMAN** is the CEO of Harrah's Entertainment and a former Harvard Business School professor. **W. EARL SASSER, JR.,** is a Baker Foundation Professor at Harvard Business School. **LEONARD A. SCHLESINGER** is the president of Babson College in Massachusetts.

Originally published in March 1994. Reprint R0807L

The Mismanagement of Customer Loyalty

by Werner Reinartz and V. Kumar

THE BEST CUSTOMERS, we're told, are loyal ones. They cost less to serve, they're usually willing to pay more than other customers, and they often act as word-of-mouth marketers for your company. Win loyalty, therefore, and profits will follow as night follows day. Certainly that's what CRM software vendors—and the armies of consultants who help install their systems—are claiming. And it seems that many business executives agree. Corporate expenditures on loyalty initiatives are booming: The top 16 retailers in Europe, for example, collectively spent more than $1 billion in 2000. Indeed, for the last ten years, the gospel of customer loyalty has been repeated so often and so loudly that it seems almost crazy to challenge it.

But that is precisely what some of the loyalty movement's early believers are starting to do. Take the case of one U.S. high-tech corporate service provider we studied. Back in 1997, this company set up an elaborate costing scheme to track the performance of its newly instituted loyalty programs. The scheme measured not only direct product costs for each customer but also all associated advertising, service, sales force, and organizational expenses. After running the scheme for five years, the company was able to determine the profitability of each of its accounts over time. Executives were curious to see just what payoff they were getting from their $2 million annual investment in customer loyalty.

The answer took them by surprise. About half of those customers who made regular purchases for at least two years—and were therefore designated as "loyal"—barely generated a profit. Conversely, about half of the most profitable customers were blow-ins, buying a great deal of high-margin products in a short time before completely disappearing.

Our research findings echo that company's experience. We've been studying the dynamics of customer loyalty using four companies' customer databases. In addition to the high-tech corporate service provider, we studied a large U.S. mail-order company, a French retail food business, and a German direct brokerage house. Collectively, the data have enabled us to compare the behavior, revenue, and profitability of more than 16,000 individual and corporate customers over a four-year period.

What we've found is that the relationship between loyalty and profitability is much weaker—and subtler— than the proponents of loyalty programs claim. Specifically, we discovered little or no evidence to suggest

Idea in Brief

"Loyal customers cost less to serve! They pay more than other customers, and attract new customers through word-of-mouth!" These loud claims prompted one high-tech service provider to launch a $2 million-per-year customer-loyalty program. Five years later, the company made disturbing discoveries: Half of its *loyal* customers barely generated a profit. And half of its most *profitable* customers bought high-margin products once—then disappeared.

What happened? As recent research reveals, the loyalty-equals-profitability equation is surprisingly weak—and complicated. Not all loyal customers are profitable, and not all profitable customers loyal.

Managing customers for loyalty doesn't automatically mean managing them for profits. To strengthen the loyalty-profitability link, you must manage both—simultaneously.

that customers who purchase steadily from a company over time are necessarily cheaper to serve, less price sensitive, or particularly effective at bringing in new business.

Indeed, in light of our findings, many companies will need to reevaluate the way they manage customer loyalty programs. Instead of focusing on loyalty alone, companies will have to find ways to measure the relationship between loyalty and profitability so that they can better identify which customers to focus on and which to ignore. Here we present one way to do that—a new methodology that will enable managers to determine far more precisely than most existing approaches do just when to let go of a given customer and so dramatically improve the returns on their investments in loyalty. We'll also discuss strategies for managing

Idea in Practice

Reconsider Customer-Loyalty Claims

A study of 16,000 customers at four companies revealed surprising findings:

Claim	Contrary finding
Loyal customers cost less to serve.	Loyal, high-volume customers know their value to you—and exploit it to get premium service and discounts.
Loyal customers pay more than other customers.	Experienced customers believe they deserve *lower* prices.
Loyal customers attract more customers through word-of-mouth.	Customers spread the word only if they *feel*, as well as *act*, loyal. To spot apostles, measure customers' attitudes as well as purchasing behavior.

Measure Loyalty—Accurately

If the loyalty-profitability link is so weak, should you abandon loyalty programs? No: The problem isn't the programs; it's the crude methods used to measure and predict loyalty. Many tools generate dangerously inaccurate information.

Example: The RFM method (recency, frequency, and monetary value) ignores pacing—time between purchases—so companies misjudge the likelihood of a customer's buying again. RFM also bases monetary value on revenue, not profitability. When customers buy only low-margin products, serving them may cost more than the revenue they generate. Results? Companies chase the wrong customers—and neglect the right ones.

relationships with customers who have different profitability and loyalty profiles. Let's begin, though, by reconsidering the evidence for the link between loyalty and profitability.

Companies need a better measurement system—one based on "event-history" modeling.

Example: By combining pacing with the average profit customers generate in typical purchase periods, an event-history approach lets marketers design effective loyalty strategies for *each* customer.

Build Loyalty Strategies

After measuring customers' profitability and predicting how long they'll remain loyal, determine in which of these four categories they fit—then tailor your strategies:

Category	Profitability/Loyalty	Loyalty Strategy
True Friends	Profitable and loyal; buy regularly but not intensively	Approach softly: Don't communicate too often, or they'll ignore everything. Reward their loyalty with exclusive access to special events and high-quality, limited-supply products.
Butterflies	Profitable but disloyal	For the short time they buy, milk them with short-term, hard-sell offers. After their purchasing drops off, stop investing.
Barnacles	Unprofitable but very loyal	If you determine they have more money to spend, offer them products related to those they've already purchased.
Strangers	Neither profitable nor loyal	Identify early. Invest nothing.

Is Loyalty Profitable?

To answer this question, we looked at the relationship between customer longevity and companies' profits. We expected to find a positive correlation, so our real question was how strong would it be. A perfect correlation (that is, 1) would mean that marketers could confidently predict exactly how much money there was to be made from retaining customers. The weaker the correlation (the closer it was to zero), the looser the association between profits and customer tenure.

The results were hardly a ringing endorsement of the loyalty mantra. The association was weak to moderate in all four companies we studied, with correlation coefficients of 0.45 for the grocery retailer, 0.30 for the corporate service provider, 0.29 for the direct brokerage firm, and just 0.20 for the mail-order company.

But did the weakness of the overall correlation between profitability and longevity conceal any truth in the specific claims about the benefits of loyal customers? To find out, we tested the three claims usually advanced by loyalty advocates, the ones we started with at the beginning of this article: that loyal customers cost less to serve, that they are willing to pay more for a given bundle of goods, and that they act as effective marketers for a company's products. We tested each of these hypotheses for all four companies by looking at several cohorts of customers at each who had begun doing business at the same time, tracking the profitability of each member of each group. In this way, we saw how these customers' purchasing patterns and the level of service the companies accorded them evolved over time.

Claim 1: It costs less to serve loyal customers

Many advocates of loyalty initiatives argue that loyal customers pay their way because the up-front costs of acquiring them are amortized over a large number of transactions. But, of course, that argument presupposes that the customers are profitable in those transactions. A more plausible argument for the link between loyalty and decreased costs can be built on the idea that loyal customers will be more familiar with a company's trans-action processes. Since they need less hand-holding, the company should find it cheaper to deal with them. Loyal—and therefore experienced—customers of soft-ware products, for example, should be able to resolve problems on-line without needing the direct interven-tion of a technical assistant.

Our analysis, however, offers no evidence to back that argument. It is certainly true that within any one company, the monthly cost of maintaining a relation-ship with an individual customer—not just for the actual transactions but also for communications through mailings, telephone, and so forth—varies enor-mously, sometimes by a factor of 100 or more. But in none of the four companies we tracked were long-standing customers consistently cheaper to manage than short-term customers. In fact, the only strong cor-relation between customer longevity and costs that we found—in the high-tech corporate service provider—suggested that loyal and presumably experienced cus-tomers were actually more expensive to serve.

That last finding isn't without precedent. There's a sizable body of academic research documenting the often poor profitability of long-standing customers in business-to-business industries. These customers, who almost invariably do business in high volumes, know their value to the company and often exploit it to get premium service or price discounts. Indeed, we discovered that in its efforts to please the regulars, the corporate service provider had developed customized Web sites for each of its top 250 clients. At the click of a button, these customers could obtain personalized service from dedicated sales and service teams. The maintenance of these teams, not to mention the Web sites, cost the company $10 million annually.

What surprised us more was the weakness of the correlation between customer loyalty and lower costs in the other three companies, where we had expected to find service costs falling over time. In the mail-order company, for example, it had seemed reasonable to assume that long-standing, experienced patrons might be happy to switch their purchases from the phone to the company's Web site, a move that would significantly reduce communication costs. Yet the communication cost-to-sales ratio for this company's long-standing clients is barely different from what it is for the newer ones; in both cases, it took a bit more than six cents (6.3 cents versus 6.5 cents, to be exact) spent on marketing communication to generate a dollar's worth of sales. It turned out that customers who processed their own orders through a Web site expected lower prices, which offset any cost savings the company may have garnered by using a cheaper channel. The disparity between the cost-to-sales ratios for recent and longtime customers at the French grocery chain and the German brokerage firm was also smaller than we had expected. At these companies, too, customers expected something in return for their loyalty.

These findings suggest that, at the very least, the link between loyalty and lower costs is industry specific. No doubt there are industries in which the oldest customers are the cheapest to serve, but as we've shown there are also others in which they are more expensive to satisfy.

Claim 2: Loyal customers pay higher prices for the same bundle of goods

If loyalty doesn't necessarily lower costs, then perhaps it generates revenue. Many proponents of the loyalty movement argue that customers who stick to one company do so because the cost of switching to another supplier is too high. They will, therefore, be willing to pay higher prices up to a point to avoid making the switch.

This argument sounds reasonable, but the logical conclusion is less obviously so—namely, that if loyal customers are worth pursuing because they'll pay higher prices, then companies will charge them higher prices. This seemed to us to be highly implausible in most corporate contexts, where customers regularly guarantee greater frequency of purchase in return for lower prices. But we did think it could describe many consumer markets. Mail-order customers, for instance, might well pay a little more for using a catalog they could find their way around. Indeed, charging established customers more is the norm in some industries. Credit card companies routinely lure in customers with promises of low initial interest rates, only to raise them later.

As we had expected, the evidence from the corporate service provider did not support the claim: The long-term customers consistently paid lower prices than the newer customers did—between 5% and 7% lower, depending on the product category. What was surprising was that we found no evidence that such loyal customers paid higher prices in the consumer businesses. Indeed, we found that like corporate clients, consumers also expect, and get, some tangible benefits for their loyalty. At the mail-order company, for instance, it turned out that regular customers actually paid 9% less than recent customers in one category of products. At the French grocery chain, there was no significant difference in prices paid in any product category. In that case, any willingness on the part of loyal customers to pay higher shelf prices was probably canceled out by the discounts many got from using the loyalty cards they were entitled to. At the brokerage house, all customers were charged the same fee—a percentage of their trade volume—regardless of their history with the company.

In general, then, it seems that a loyal customer—whether corporate or consumer—is actually more price sensitive than an occasional one. A number of theories could explain this phenomenon. First, loyal customers generally are more knowledgeable about product offerings and can better assess their quality. That means they can develop solid reference prices and make better judgments about value than sporadic customers can. This was certainly in evidence at the mail-order company; loyal customers typically would choose cheaper product alternatives—a lower-priced blender, say—in the catalogs than would those who were less familiar with the company.

Perhaps more fundamental, though, is the fact that customers seem to strongly resent companies that try to profit from loyalty. Surveys consistently report that consumers believe loyal customers deserve lower prices. This may well explain why U.S. telecom companies, which routinely offer customers special deals initially only to raise prices later, all experience high rates of customer churn. Finally, it's just plain impossible these days to get away with price differentiation for any length of time. Remember how close Amazon came to destroying its brand when it attempted to charge different prices to different customers for the same DVDs.

Claim 3: Loyal customers market the company

The idea that the more frequent customers are also the strongest advocates for your company holds a great attraction for marketers. Word-of-mouth marketing is supremely effective, of course, and many companies justify their investments in loyalty programs by seeking profits not so much from the loyal customers as from the new customers the loyal ones bring in.

To test whether regular customers of the French grocery chain were actually more effective marketers than infrequent customers, we asked a sample of the company's customers two questions. First, to gauge the extent of passive word-of-mouth marketing, we inquired whether they named the company when asked to recommend a particular grocery retailer. Then, to measure the level of active word-of-mouth marketing, we asked whether they ever spontaneously told friends or family about positive experiences with the company. We then identified every customer's actual level of loyalty, as measured by his or her recorded purchase behavior (that is, how often, how much, and how many different sorts of items were purchased). Finally, we solicited their own subjective measure of loyalty, their "attitudinal loyalty," in a telephone survey, in which we asked them if they felt loyal to the company, how satisfied they were with it, and whether they had any interest in switching to another company.

Overall, the link between customer longevity and the propensity to market by word-of-mouth was not that strong. But when we looked at attitudinal and actual loyalty separately, the results were intriguing. Customers of the grocery chain who scored high on both loyalty measures were 54% more likely to be active word-of-mouth marketers and 33% more likely to be passive word-of-mouth marketers than those who scored high on behavioral loyalty alone. The results from a survey of the corporate service provider's customers produced similar if less striking results: Customers who exhibited high levels of both behavioral and attitudinal loyalty were 44% more likely to be active marketers and 26% more likely to be passive word-of-mouth marketers.

Although it's perhaps not surprising that people who talk more positively about a company are also more likely to sell others on the company, our findings are important for loyalty managers because most measure loyalty purely on the basis of purchasing behavior and do not conduct attitudinal surveys like ours. But if managers are investing in a loyalty program for its supposed marketing benefits, then they are looking at a potentially misleading indicator. Customers may well buy all their groceries at the same supermarket out of inertia and convenience. To identify the true apostles, companies need to judge customers by more than just their actions.

Knowing When to Lose a Customer

Our empirical findings are clear-cut. The link between loyalty and profits is weaker than expected, and none of the usual justifications for investing in loyalty stands up well to examination. But that doesn't mean we believe investments in loyalty are doomed. In our opinion, the reason the link between loyalty and profits is weak has a lot to do with the crudeness of the methods most companies currently use to decide whether or not to maintain their customer relationships.

The most common way to sort customers is to score them according to how often they make purchases and how much they spend. Many tools do that; one of the most familiar is called RFM (which stands for *recency, frequency,* and *monetary value*). Mail-order companies in particular, including the one in our study, rely on this tool to assess whether a customer relationship merits further investment.

To understand how RFM and methods like it work, let's imagine for the sake of simplicity that a company focuses on just two dimensions, recency and frequency of purchase. This company measures recency by finding out from its database if the customer bought something in the last six months, between six months and a year ago, or more than a year ago, assigning a higher score the more recent the purchase. It then measures how frequently the customer made purchases in each of those three time frames—twice or more, once, or never—assigning a score in a similar way. Then it adds the two scores together. In general, the more items a customer purchases and the more recent the transactions, the higher the overall score and the more resources the company lavishes on the person. In actual application, many companies weight the scores in favor of recency.

Unfortunately, our study of the mail-order company suggests that scoring approaches of this kind result in a significant overinvestment in lapsed customers. Take a look at the graph "The Cost of Keeping Customers On." It plots the profits earned from one particular segment of customers—those who turned out to have purchased very intensively for a brief period and then never again. The profits from those customers were tracked for 36 months—the full time the company treated them as active customers because their initial high volume of purchases kept their RFM scores high even after they'd stopped buying. As the graph shows, the company started to incur losses on these customers after about 20 months. We estimate that the total cost to the company of misinvestments of this kind amounted to about $1 million a year.

So just why is RFM such a poor way to measure loyalty? One problem is that patterns of buying behavior for

The cost of keeping customers on

Just because a group of customers was profitable in the past doesn't mean it will continue to be so in the future. Many nonloyal customers can be very profitable initially, causing companies to chase after them in vain for future profits. Such is the case illustrated in this graph, which tracks the profitability of that segment of one company's customers. Once these customers ceased their buying activity, they became unprofitable because the company kept investing in marketing to them.

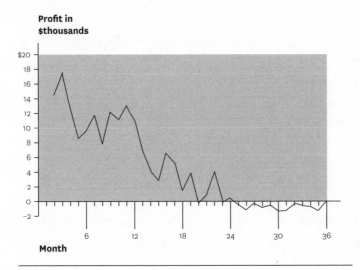

frequently bought goods are quite different than those for infrequently bought goods. But RFM can't distinguish between them—that is, it ignores the pacing of a customer's interactions, the time between each purchase. To understand the importance of pacing, imagine that your company has two hypothetical customers—Mr. Smith and Ms. Jones—who both start to buy goods in month one. Over the course of the first year, they purchase at different rates: Smith buys after short intervals, making purchases again in the second, sixth, and eighth months, whereas Jones takes far longer to buy again, waiting a full seven months before she purchases again in month eight.

A simple RFM evaluation might suggest that Smith is likely to be more loyal than Jones—his purchases are more frequent and as recent and thus more deserving of investment. But an RFM evaluation would fail to take into account the fact that Smith usually buys something, on average, every 2.3 months, and yet by month 12 he hasn't bought anything for four months. Jones, too, hasn't bought anything for four months. But she normally doesn't buy anything for seven months, so she's well within her historic range. On that basis, the probability that Jones will purchase in the future is actually higher than it is for Smith, so she is more likely to be a safe bet for further investment.

The model of buying behavior we're describing here is a special case of "event-history modeling," a statistical technique with a long and strong history. Like most statistical models, it figures the probability that some future event will occur based on statistical patterns observed either theoretically or empirically in the past. Other examples of event-history modeling are the occurrence of hurricanes over time and the recurrence of diseases within a population. In our case, the "event" is purchasing, and the past patterns are taken from the empirical data our four companies have collected in their customer databases.

There are more and less complex ways to use the event-history model to compute the probability that a customer will keep on purchasing. But in its simplest form, the formula is t^n, where, for Smith in our example, n is the number of purchases he made in the entire time period (in this case, the whole year), and t is the fraction of the period represented by the time between his first purchase and his last one.

Let's use the formula to assess the probabilities that Smith and Jones will each remain active, that is, keep on making purchases. Smith has made four purchases, the last being in month eight, so n is 4 and t is 8 ÷ 12 or 0.6667. That makes Smith's probability of still being active $(0.6667)^4$, or 0.198. In other words, there's about a 20% probability that Smith will keep on purchasing. Jones also made her last purchase in month eight, so her t is 0.6667 as well, but she bought only twice, so her probability is $(0.6667)^2$, or 0.444, nearly 45%. Jones, therefore, is more than twice as likely as Smith to remain an active customer. Unlike RFM, this approach is particularly good at predicting how quickly a customer's purchasing activity will drop off, as the probability of their being active in the future drops steeply with time, so it clearly has the potential to prevent heavy overinvestment in profitable but disloyal customers.

In practice, of course, our calculations are much more sophisticated than the foregoing example and can take into account any number of variables, including demographics, amount of spending, and type of products purchased.[1] Given enough historical data, we can estimate the probability of another purchase out into several future time periods. But no matter how complex the software a company uses to do the math, the analysis is very easy to implement, since all such probability models depend on just three simple pieces of information that any customer database stores: When did the customer buy for the first time? When did she purchase last? and When did she purchase in between?

The second main drawback of scoring methods like RFM is that the monetary-value component is almost always based on revenue rather than profitability. For example, the mail-order company classifies the revenue generated from a customer into the following four categories: $50 or less, $51 to $150, $151 to $300, and more than $300. But the decision to continue investing in customer relationships needs to be based on customers' profitability, not the revenue they generate. The cost of servicing customers who buy only small quantities of low-margin products may exceed the revenue they bring in. That profile turned out to fit fully 29% of the mail-order company's customers.

Instead of looking at revenue, therefore, we will need to incorporate profitability into our probability calculation. Specifically, we need an estimate of the average profit earned on each customer in any typical purchase period. For Smith and Jones, that's the average monthly profit figure, but the choice of the time period is generally driven by an industry's natural purchase cycle. In the mail-order business, marketers think in terms of months or quarters. In retailing, the period is a week.

An estimate of per-period profitability is not hard to obtain, especially in today's information-rich age. Our corporate high-tech service provider, for example, was easily able to calculate the historical profitability of each of its customers from its sales data, and we have been able to calculate the profitability of individual customers for the other companies we studied as well. To estimate a customer's future profitability, you simply multiply his average periodic profit figure by the number we previously calculated, the probability that the customer will still be active at the end of that period.

To see how this works, consider how a simple version of our approach could help the high-tech corporate service provider decide whether and how to invest in two ongoing customer relationships during the next year. From its sales data, the provider determines that the first account, Adam Incorporated, yielded an average profit of $5,500 per quarter over the last two years, while the second account, Eve Limited, yielded an average profit of $1,000. Using the formula, we estimate the probability that Adam Incorporated will remain active is 85% in the first quarter, 60% in the second, 35% in the third, and only 22% in the fourth. Probabilities for Eve Limited are only slightly lower, starting at 80% in the first quarter and declining to 50%, 27%, and 15% in the subsequent quarters. For each account, we now multiply the probability figure for each period by the historical average profit number, and the sum of those calculations gives us the estimated profit in dollars for each customer over the next year.

Which customers are really profitable?

When customers are sorted according to their profitability and longevity, it becomes clear that the relationship between loyalty and profits is by no means assured. Here, a sizable percentage of long-standing customers in all four companies are only marginally profitable, whereas a large percentage of short-term customers are highly profitable. It is these segments that drive down the overall correlation between loyalty and profitability.

	Short-term customers Percentage of customers	Long-term customers Percentage of customers
High profitability		
corporate service provider	20%	30%
grocery retail	15%	36%
mail-order	19%	31%
direct brokerage	18%	32%
Low profitability		
corporate service provider	29%	21%
grocery retail	34%	15%
mail-order	29%	21%
direct brokerage	33%	17%

Both accounts are clearly profitable: Adam Incorporated is likely to generate $11,110, while Eve Limited will likely produce $1,720. But how much should the company invest in maintaining each relationship so that it will actually deliver the numbers? Given that a visit by the full sales team costs our company $5,000 and a single sales-person's visit costs $2,000, it's clear that Adam Incorporated merits the full treatment. Eve Limited, however, doesn't deserve even a single visit. If the account stays active, that's obviously good news, but it's not worth our company's time to chase the sale. Even loyal and profitable customers don't always deserve to be courted.

When tested on real customer databases, our approach produced a nuanced picture of the relationship between profitability and loyalty. About 40% of the service provider's profitable customers turned out to be not worth chasing, being unlikely to buy anything in the future, and almost the same percentage of the loyal ones were unprofitable. Fully 30% turned out to be neither profitable nor loyal. (See our results for all four companies in the chart "Which Customers Are Really Profitable?").

As valuable as segmentation is, even more valuable is correct identification at the individual level. Knowing that 60% of your loyal customers are profitable is useless if you don't know which ones to court with what level of service. At the corporate service provider, for example, we were able to predict how profitable and how loyal any particular customer would be with 30% more accuracy than we obtained using traditional methods like RFM. That kind of misinformation carries a high price. Our mail-order company, for instance, was sending mailings to people it should have ignored, ignoring people it should have been cultivating, and sending the wrong material to people.

From Measurement to Management

So what is the next step? After analyzing your customers' profitability and the projected duration of their relationships, you can place each of them into one of four categories, as shown in the matrix "Choosing a

---

Choosing a loyalty strategy

When profitability and loyalty are considered at the same time, it becomes clear that different customers need to be treated in different ways.

	Butterflies	**True Friends**
High profitability	• good fit between company's offerings and customers' needs • high profit potential *Actions:* • aim to achieve transactional satisfaction, not attitudinal loyalty • milk the accounts only as long as they are active • key challenge is to cease investing soon enough	• good fit between company's offerings and customers' needs • high profit potential *Actions:* • communicate consistently but not too often • build both attitudinal and behavioral loyalty • delight these customers to nurture, defend, and retain them
	Strangers	**Barnacles**
Low profitability	• little fit between company's offerings and customers' needs • lowest profit potential *Actions:* • make no investment in these relationships • make profit on every transaction	• limited fit between company's offerings and customers' needs • low profit potential *Actions:* • measure both the size and share of wallet • if share of wallet is low, focus on up- and cross-selling • if size of wallet is small, impose strict cost controls
	Short-term customers	Long-term customers

Loyalty Strategy." Now, what kind of relationship management strategies should you apply to the different segments? For the customers who have no loyalty and bring in no profits—we call them "strangers"—the answer is simple: Identify early and don't invest anything. But for customers in the other three quadrants, the choice of strategy will make a material difference to the segment's profitability.

We've found that the challenge in managing customers who are profitable but disloyal—the "butterflies"—is to milk them for as much as you can for the short time they are buying from you. A softly-softly approach is more appropriate for profitable customers who are likely to be loyal—your "true friends." As for highly loyal but not very profitable customers—the "barnacles"—the emphasis has to be on finding out whether they have the potential to spend more than they currently do.

Turning True Friends into True Believers

Profitable, loyal customers are usually satisfied with existing arrangements. At the mail-order company, for instance, we found that they tended to return goods at a relatively high rate, reflecting their comfort in engaging with the company's processes. They are also steady purchasers, buying regularly, but not intensively, over time.

In managing these true friends, the greatest trap is overkill. At the catalog company, for instance, we found that intensifying the level of contact through, for example, increased mailings, was more likely to put off loyal and profitable customers than to increase sales. People flooded with mail may throw everything out without looking at it. Sent less mail, however, they are more likely to look at what they get. Indeed, the mail-order company found that its profitable, loyal customers were not among those who received the most mailings.

What's more, companies need to concentrate on finding ways to bring to the fore their true friends' feelings of loyalty, because "true believers" are the most valuable customers of all. At the grocery retailer, for example, we found that customers who scored high on both actual and attitudinal measures of loyalty generated 120% more profit than those whose loyalty was observed through transactions alone. It wasn't just a business-to-consumer phenomenon, either: Those of the corporate service provider's customers who exhibited loyalty in both thought and deed were 50% more profitable than those who expressed their loyalty through action alone.

Companies can do several things to make loyal customers feel rewarded for their loyalty. The French grocery chain lets loyal customers opt in to e-mailings of special recipes, price promotions, and the like. It also grants them preferred access to company-sponsored seasonal events. For instance, they get exclusive early access to semiannual, weeklong wine festivals in which they get to buy many of the better wines, which are available only in limited quantities. Such measures are already having an appreciable impact on the purchasing volumes and profitability of loyal customers.

Enjoying Butterflies

The next most valuable group comprises customers who are profitable but transient, and some industries are full of these kinds of purchasers. For instance, many of the direct brokerage company's most valuable customers were what it called "movers," investors who trade shares often and in large amounts. Aware of their value as customers, these people enjoy hunting out the best deals, and they avoid building a stable relationship with any single provider.

The classic mistake made in managing these accounts is continuing to invest in them after their activity drops off. Any such efforts are almost invariably wasted; our research shows that attempts to convert butterflies into loyal customers are seldom successful—the conversion rate was 10% or lower for each of the four companies we studied. Instead of treating butterflies as potential true believers, therefore, managers should look for ways to enjoy them while they can and find the right moment to cease investing in them. In practice, this usually means a short-term hard sell through promotions and mailing blitzes that include special offers on other products, an approach that might well irritate loyal customers. The corporate service provider, for instance, telephones those it has identified as butterflies four or five times shortly after their most recent purchase and follows up with just one direct mailing six to 12 months later, depending on the product category. If these communications bear no fruit, the company drops contact altogether.

Smoothing Barnacles

These customers are the most problematic. They do not generate satisfactory returns on investments made in account maintenance and marketing because the size and volume of their transactions are too low. Like barnacles on the hull of a cargo ship, they only create additional drag. Properly managed, though, they can sometimes become profitable.

The first step is to determine whether the problem is a small wallet (the customers aren't valuable to begin with and are not worth chasing) or a small share of the wallet (they could spend more and should be chased). Thanks to modern information technology, which makes it possible to record the spending patterns of individuals, this is much less of a challenge than it once was. Our French grocery chain, in fact, does it rather well. By looking closely at POS data on the type and amount of products that individuals purchase (say, baby or pet food), the company derives amazingly reliable estimates of the size and share of the individual customers' wallets it has already captured in each product category. Then, a company can easily distinguish which loyal customers are potentially profitable and offer them products associated with those already purchased, as well as certain other items in seemingly unrelated categories. For instance, our corporate service provider might sell add-on software or memory upgrades for previously sold systems. Our mail-order company might send a do-it-yourself catalog to a customer who had previously bought a kitchen appliance.

There is no one right way to make loyalty profitable. Different approaches will be more suitable to different businesses, depending on the profiles of their customers and the complexity of their distribution channels. But whatever the context, we believe that no company should ever take for granted the idea that managing customers for loyalty is the same as managing them for profits. The only way to strengthen the link between profits and loyalty is to manage both at the same time. Fortunately, technology is making that task easier every day, allowing companies to record and analyze the often complex, and sometimes even perverse, behavior of their customers.

Note

1. A complete explanation of the actual model we use can be found in our article, "On the Profitability of Long-Life Customers in a Noncontractual Setting: An Empirical Investigation and Implications for Marketing," *Journal of Marketing* (October 2000).

WERNER REINARTZ is an assistant professor of marketing at Insead in France. **V. KUMAR** is the ING Chair Professor at the University of Connecticut's School of Business.

Originally published in July 2002. Reprint R0207F

CRM Done Right

by Darrell K. Rigby and Dianne Ledingham

THROUGH THE LATE 1990S AND into 2000, managers plowed millions of dollars into information systems meant to track and strengthen customer relationships. Often built around complex software packages, these customer relationship management (CRM) systems promised to allow companies to respond efficiently, and at times instantly, to shifting customer desires, thereby bolstering revenues and retention while reducing marketing costs. But most firms failed to reap the expected benefits, and as executives dramatically reduced IT expenses in subsequent years, CRM sales plummeted. After rising 28% between 1999 and 2000, CRM sales dropped by 5% in 2001, 25% in 2002, and 17% in 2003, according to the technology market research firm Gartner. Many observers came to believe that CRM was destined to join enterprise resource planning (ERP) as another overhyped IT investment whose initial unmet promise nearly killed off the approach.

But something unexpected has happened: Senior executives have become considerably more enthusiastic about CRM. In 2003, Bain & Company's annual

Management Tools Survey of 708 global executives found that firms actually began to report increased satisfaction with their CRM investments. In 2001, CRM had ranked near the bottom of a list of 25 possible tools global executives would choose. Two years later, it had moved into the top half. In fact, 82% of surveyed executives said they planned to employ CRM in their companies in 2003—a large jump from the 35% who employed it in 2000. Today, CRM spending appears to be picking up. Gartner forecasts that overall CRM sales will rise another 10% by the end of 2005. So what's changed? Why has disappointment turned to satisfaction, pessimism to optimism, cutbacks to new spending?

To answer these questions, we studied a wide range of companies that have recently been successful in implementing CRM systems, and we discovered some common threads in their experiences. Most important, they've all taken a pragmatic, disciplined approach to CRM, launching highly focused projects that are relatively narrow in their scope and modest in their goals. Rather than use CRM to transform entire businesses, they've directed their investments toward solving clearly defined problems within their customer relationship cycle—the series of activities that runs from the initial segmenting and targeting of customers all the way through to wooing them back for more.

The successful users have also exhibited a healthy skepticism, discounting overblown claims that the ultimate payback from a CRM system is the creation of a "real-time enterprise." Understanding that highly accurate and timely data are not required everywhere

Idea in Brief

Disappointed by the high costs and elusive benefits, early adopters of customer relationship management systems came, in the post dot-com era, to view the technology as just another overhyped IT investment whose initial promise would never be fulfilled. But this year, something unexpected is happening. System sales are rising, and executives are reporting satisfaction with their CRM investments. What's changed? A wide range of companies are successfully taking a pragmatic, disciplined approach to CRM. Rather than use it to transform entire businesses, they've directed their investments toward solving clearly defined problems within their customer relationship cycle. The authors have distilled the experiences of these CRM leaders into four questions that all companies should ask themselves as they launch their own CRM initiatives: Is the problem strategic? Is the system focused on the pain point? Do we need perfect data? What's the right way to expand an initial implementation? The questions reflect a new realism about when and how to deploy CRM to its best advantage. Understanding that highly accurate and timely data are not required everywhere in their businesses, CRM leaders have tailored their real-time initiatives to those customer relationships that can be significantly enhanced by "perfect" information. After they've succeeded with their first targeted CRM project, they can use it as a springboard for solving additional problems. CRM, in other words, is coming to resemble any other valuable management tool, and the keys to successful implementation are also becoming familiar: strong executive and business unit leadership, careful strategic planning, clear performance measures, and a coordinated program that combines organizational and process changes with the application of new technology.

in their businesses, they've tailored their real-time CRM initiatives to those parts of their customer relationships that truly do depend on "perfect" information. Once they've succeeded with the smaller, more-targeted CRM project, they've used their initial investments as springboards for solving additional problems.

We've distilled the experiences of the CRM leaders into four questions that all companies should ask themselves as they launch their CRM initiatives:

- Is it strategic?

- Where does it hurt?

- Do we need perfect data?

- Where do we go from here?

The questions reflect a new realism about when and how to deploy CRM to its best advantage. When Darrell Rigby, Fred Reichheld, and Phil Schefter took stock of CRM's effectiveness in these pages nearly three years ago (in "Avoid the Four Perils of CRM," February 2002), lots of companies were still placing big bets that the technology would pay off—somehow. Lacking clear customer strategies and the organizational structures to support them, many firms got burned and grew distrustful of CRM. The difficult lessons such organizations learned have led them to sharpen their customer strategies, setting the stage for real gains from more-focused CRM applications.

In this article, we'll show how several companies have implemented successful CRM efforts—aircraft parts distributor Aviall, consumer product giant Kimberly-Clark, diversified equipment maker Ingersoll-Rand, home- and office-machine company Brother International, and electronic connector manufacturer Molex. We'll also lay out some basic considerations that can help firms determine which CRM projects are likely to yield the most value.

Is It Strategic?

There's no getting around it: A CRM program involves complicated business and technology issues and requires significant investments of time and money. CRM is not a tool for buffing a company's performance at the edges; it should be applied only to processes vital to a company's competitiveness—those that can distance a firm from its competitors or keep a function (such as call center response time) on par with the rest of the industry when parity counts. If the target is not truly strategic, the organization will be hard-pressed to summon the vigor necessary to tackle entrenched business processes or retool its organizational structure and garner expected returns. Before spending a dime on CRM, therefore, executives need to make sure they have the right targets in their sights.

Paul Fulchino knew the stakes involved when he brought CRM into Aviall after being appointed CEO in 2000. Fulchino had ambitious plans to transform the Dallas-based distributor of aircraft parts into the premier vendor of supply chain management services to the aviation industry. By becoming the preferred partner of both the big original equipment manufacturers (OEMs) and the commercial and military fleet owners, Aviall could consolidate customer demand and extend its reach worldwide, which would reinvigorate its sales and strengthen its margins.

But Fulchino faced a daunting obstacle to realizing his vision: Poor information and cumbersome processes hampered the company's sales and service operation. Difficulties with an existing IT system had increased sales reps' workloads, sometimes keeping salespeople trapped in local branches, helping managers input order information instead of making sales calls. What's more, the company hadn't trained the sales reps in proper time and territory management, which led to inefficient phone call routing and haphazard calling schedules. Customer inquiries were often routed to distant call centers that lacked up-to-date data on orders, products, and prices.

The weak customer service left key accounts vulnerable to competitors' attacks and undermined the company's ability to charge the premium prices typically associated with flawless product delivery. A better-trained and more proactive sales force was a strategic necessity. Without one, Fulchino's aggressive plans for the company would go unfulfilled. So the new CEO, working closely with his sales and marketing head, Jim Quinn, and his technology chief, Joe Lacik, dedicated Aviall's initial CRM outlays to this critical challenge. Rather than attempt a full-scale implementation of a broad CRM program, the executives took a more focused approach, installing only the sales force, order entry, and call center applications to begin with. Their goal was to coordinate customer information seamlessly from the outside sales agents, first to the inside sales support staff, then to the customer service representatives who were manning the company's 36 regional call centers. The relatively narrow focus allowed the sales force to become familiar with the system without being overwhelmed and delivered quick victories that helped win broader management and line support and gather momentum behind the project.

The gains were striking. Before having the CRM system, the sales force relied on an outmoded database for managing client information. The system's inflexibility made it difficult for sales and service staffers to get even basic information on a customer's order history and credit status. "There's nothing more frustrating than having a customer spend 15 minutes on an order and then realizing at the very end that there's a credit issue," says Lacik. "In the old system, credit problems didn't get flagged until you tried to place the order. Then the credit group would be called in, and you either had to have the customer on hold for a long time or call them back. In our business, there's a moment of truth: You have to have the right product, the right information, and the right price. If you don't have those three things put together, you lose the call—and if you lose the call, 90% of the time you lose the sale." With the new system, a customer's credit history instantly popped up on the order screen.

The rich information the new system provided allowed Jim Quinn to flip a switch in the sales force. It helped the agents get organized and spurred them to make more customer calls, knowing they could immediately deliver firm quotes on tailored sets of products or services. Placing an order had once required them to go through 11 screens and nearly 50 steps; now they could do it with one screen and ten steps. Just four months into rolling out the CRM system, the number of daily sales calls tripled, and the customer base grew by 33%. In fact, the productivity of the entire sales and service operation skyrocketed, helping Aviall recapture market share and win large orders for new product lines. The number of orders handled per day jumped from 1,000 to 2,500, even as error rates declined, with no increase in staff.

The expanded capacity, together with the improvements in service, have built the platform the company needed to reshape itself as a full-service provider of aviation logistics support. Aviall's sales and profits have grown rapidly, and it has steadily stolen market share from competitors. In a testament to Aviall's success, engine maker Rolls-Royce recently awarded the firm a ten-year supply contract worth $3 billion—the largest deal ever struck by any company in the industry. Says CIO Lacik: "We showed Rolls-Royce the level of visibility we had into our customer base—visibility that we could share with them to give them a deeper understanding of customer buying trends and behavior. . . . A simple analysis showed Rolls-Royce that it had several years' worth of supply in some products while being understocked in others because it was not matching manufacturing adequately with customer demand. That was a pivotal moment in winning the contract." Tightly focused on a single area of critical strategic importance, CRM has become a linchpin of Aviall's reinvention.

Where Does It Hurt?

It's possible to use CRM systems to manage the entire customer relationship cycle all at once—initial purchase, after-sales service, subsequent purchases, recommendations to other customers (for the full range of functions a CRM system can automate, see the exhibit, "The Customer Relationship Cycle"). But as the most aggressive early adopters found, that's usually a bad idea. Such an approach ends up creating unused technology capacity, causes unnecessary business disruptions, and ultimately fails the payback test. When companies carefully examine their customer relationship cycles, they usually find some deep-seated, pernicious problems in a few areas that undermine overall performance. It is these pain points that should be the focus of the CRM effort.

For Kimberly-Clark, one of the world's leading consumer packaged-goods companies, the pain point lay in its vast retailer promotions operation. The manufacturer was running thousands of promotions every year, usually offering a discount on a particular product to a particular retailer, but it was unable to accurately gauge the success of any of them. The firm had aggregate numbers on its trade promotions, but it couldn't break them down by individual customer, product, or shipment. As a result, Kimberly-Clark found itself spending huge quantities of marketing dollars, uncertain which promotions were producing retailer loyalty, shelf space, and sales, and which were going to waste.

The customer relationship cycle

A comprehensive CRM system can, in theory, automate every aspect of a company's relationship with its customers, from all the activities needed to target customers through those for product development, sales, service, and retention. But smart companies sharply focus their CRM implementations, carefully choosing which segment of the cycle, and which functions within that segment, are likely to deliver the greatest return on an initial CRM investment. Success with this first effort often lights the way to subsequent projects—automating additional functions in the same segment (as Kimberly-Clark did), steadily moving from segment to segment (as Brother did), or even moving to critical business processes beyond CRM (as Molex did).

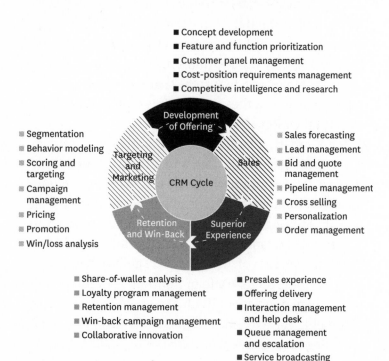

■ Concept development
■ Feature and function prioritization
■ Customer panel management
■ Cost-position requirements management
■ Competitive intelligence and research

※ Segmentation
※ Behavior modeling
※ Scoring and targeting
※ Campaign management
※ Pricing
※ Promotion
※ Win/loss analysis

Development of Offering

Targeting and Marketing

Sales

CRM Cycle

Retention and Win-Back

Superior Experience

※ Sales forecasting
※ Lead management
※ Bid and quote management
※ Pipeline management
※ Cross selling
※ Personalization
※ Order management

■ Share-of-wallet analysis
■ Loyalty program management
■ Retention management
■ Win-back campaign management
■ Collaborative innovation

■ Presales experience
■ Offering delivery
■ Interaction management and help desk
■ Queue management and escalation
■ Service broadcasting

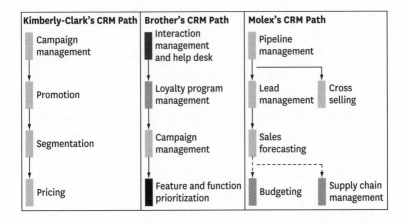

Kimberly-Clark's CRM Path	Brother's CRM Path	Molex's CRM Path	
Campaign management	Interaction management and help desk	Pipeline management	
Promotion	Loyalty program management	Lead management	Cross selling
Segmentation	Campaign management	Sales forecasting	
Pricing	Feature and function prioritization	Budgeting	Supply chain management

Company executives therefore reasoned that starting with a modest, customized CRM system to collect and analyze promotion data could substantially improve the effectiveness of its overall customer relationship cycle.

Kimberly-Clark started by building onto an existing software program for account management, called Profit Calculator, which its sales department had developed to track investments in individual promotion efforts. By integrating that with shipment data, the enhanced system could go beyond just providing general information about whether ROI was positive or negative. It could more precisely measure the impact of a particular promotion on sales and profits for both Kimberly-Clark and its retailer customers. Says Bruce Paynter, Kimberly-Clark's vice president for customer development: "Now we can see what the real-time impact on our sales and profit is when running promotions. Moreover, we can integrate this information into our sales and planning process with our customer." Renamed Business Planner, the software became the heart of the company's sales and marketing efforts: salespeople used the tool in the field to design promotional packages for specific retailers, while the company's marketing staff used it to plot broader promotion plans.

Rolled out to all of Kimberly-Clark's businesses in 2000, and supported by intensive training programs led by the organization's top executives, Business Planner rapidly proved a success. In its first year, the system was used to manage more than 2,300 promotional events involving all of the company's U.S. consumer product lines. "We applied real-time promotional-lift models [models of just how much a given promotion can lift sales] at the market, customer, and category level to aid our planning efforts with customers," Paynter says. "Using the knowledge gained through the Business Planner, we have been able to redirect $30 million in marketing spending across all our U.S. consumer businesses to drive incremental sales and profit and further build brand for our customers and Kimberly-Clark."

Equally important, managers say, Business Planner armed customer representatives with consistent data and business rules, which has broadened their perspective. Rather than think purely of managing sales, they think in terms of managing the business. Today, key-account reps can assess likely financial results and engage in scenario planning jointly with retailers.

And their effectiveness in reducing pain in trade promotions has revealed new opportunities. Building on the success of its Business Planner software, Kimberly-Clark is now implementing a more ambitious system designed to reach beyond its retailer customers into a wide array of consumer-advertising and promotional activities. The enhanced suite, coined Brand Builder, helps the company plan and evaluate the success of individual activities—a freestanding coupon inserted into the Sunday papers, for instance—and measure the combined effect of a number of integrated activities.

The Brand Builder suite comprises three related components: It includes a state-of-the-art collaborative tool that lets sales agents, designers, vendors, and retailers plan promotions online. It puts marketing research and information learned about consumers online in real time. And by integrating promotional-spending data with scanner and financial information, it provides a powerful analytical tool. In fact, with the new analysis tool, Kimberly-Clark has moved from relieving a pain point for its retailer customers to making a science of marketing. The company now knows, for example, that the payback for some consumer promotion programs is twice as high as for others intended to produce the same results. With that kind of information, the firm can identify which elements of marketing—coupon value or creative impact, for instance—result in higher returns.

Focusing on pain points can not only be an effective way to build a successful CRM program but can also get an unsuccessful CRM initiative back on track. That was true for Ingersoll-Rand, the $10 billion diversified manufacturer.

In 2001, Club Car, the Ingersoll-Rand division that makes motorized golf carts, or "golf cars" as the company calls them, was showing signs of trouble, with

Routine aches versus strategic pain points

Doctors commonly distinguish between routine aches ("Take two aspirin and call me in the morning") and perilous pains ("Meet me at the hospital in five minutes!"). Likewise, successful CRM practitioners have learned to distinguish between routine aches in the business ("Perhaps we might address that issue in our next five-year plan") and strategic pain points ("Fixing this problem will double our profits") before prescribing CRM solutions. Addressing strategic pain points typically promises superior financial rewards and the opportunity to build vital momentum for CRM programs. Here's how to identify them:

Routine aches	Strategic pain points
The problem is well known but minor, even though it affects some vociferous customers.	The problem is sometimes hidden but has a critical impact on the satisfaction and loyalty of the most valuable customers.
Solutions are quickly and easily copied by any competitor.	Solving the problem creates a substantial and sustainable competitive advantage.
The problem could have been fixed long ago without a CRM system.	Solving the problem cost effectively requires the speed, accuracy, and effectiveness of CRM technologies.
Solving the problem is not vital to the organization or its culture.	The solution will become a rallying point for the organization.
Solving the problem would fix one immediate problem.	Solving the problem would create important new capabilities that would open up additional opportunities.
Solving the problem would deliver soft, unquantifiable benefits.	Solving the problem would deliver tangible financial returns that would justify further investment—even in difficult times.
Solving the problem would not make much of a splash in the organization.	Solving the problem would represent a highly marketable success, both inside and outside the company.

revenues beginning to drift downward as an economic downturn hit the golf industry. But management lacked the information needed to diagnose the reasons for the slowing sales. Individual reps and order managers used their own idiosyncratic processes for dealing with customers. Sales forecasts were made informally using guesswork and rudimentary spreadsheets, and the sales force had little influence over product customization.

Realizing it needed much better information, Ingersoll-Rand rushed to roll out a broad CRM system that was supposed to incorporate everything from lead evaluation to proposal generation and from product configuration to order entry. But the effort proved too much for the organization to digest. Club Car's managers weren't convinced of the ultimate benefits. After spending more than $2 million and completing a first round of user testing, the company discovered that the system wasn't delivering the anticipated productivity gains and reporting capabilities. In fact, the system would dramatically increase the administrative workload of the field sales reps instead of freeing them to spend more time with customers. The unit's president had the foresight to halt the effort and made the organization back up and refine its goals. Club Car's management team took a fresh look at the key processes in its customer relationship cycle and refocused its CRM initiative on the two deepest pain points: forecasting sales and taking orders.

Today, just two years after the CRM effort was relaunched, Club Car has successfully automated its sales operation, significantly improving both customer service and business decision making. By more directly involving the sales force in the redesign of the system, carefully paring down the data and processes it encompassed, and improving the underlying technology, the company eliminated many of the CRM system's original drawbacks. Sales reps use the new system at customers' sites to modify the cars with them, and for the first time, the reps can see the financial implications of different configurations before setting prices and delivery dates. The order information the reps collect is automatically combined with general industry data on golf cart demand and equipment replacement cycles to generate reliable sales forecasts. That, in turn, has led to smoother, more predictable manufacturing schedules.

Do We Need Perfect Data?

Part of the early attraction of CRM systems lay in their ability to deliver real-time information—to give marketers, salespeople, and managers a clear picture of what's happening in the market at any particular moment. But perfect information comes at a high cost. The systems required to collect and disseminate it are expensive; so are the finely tuned processes needed to react quickly to it. Despite the hype surrounding real-time enterprises, the fact is that few companies need perfect information throughout their customer relationship cycles.

Why pay for real-time information on business processes that customers don't really value or that managers can't rapidly adjust? A hotel manager certainly needs real-time data on the availability of rooms but not on the customer's opinion of the carpets and drapes. A cable company needs real-time figures on service outages that demand immediate repairs but not on the profitability of its pay-per-view programs. Real-time information priorities are driven by real-time business opportunities and must be customized to each individual business. (See the sidebar "Calculating the Cost of CRM.")

Companies need to clearly distinguish between activities that truly demand perfect data and those that can get by with "good enough" information. The requirements for each are quite different. The approach Brother International took to its CRM implementation is a good case in point. The U.S.-based distribution arm of the Japanese maker of typewriters, printers, fax-printer-copiers, and sewing machines, Brother International faced a persistent problem: a high rate of product returns. A leading cause of the returns, the company believed, was dissatisfaction with service from its call center. In the late 1990s, as office products became more sophisticated, end users began to require more assistance. But Brother's call centers were answering only 46% of the queries coming in from new purchasers, and the quality of the help provided varied widely. Service representatives were failing to address recent buyers' questions and complaints. In particular, call center staffers lacked accurate customer information and quick access to solutions for callers' problems. To help customers troubleshoot technical issues, staffers often had to search through binders of product information. Frustrated consumers were returning their products to retailers.

Here, Brother's executives saw, was a pain point that could be remedied only through the provision of "perfect" information; they therefore looked to CRM to bolster their call centers. The company rolled out the new system in stages, starting with the printer call center in

Calculating the Cost of CRM

WITH CLEAR THINKING AND a basic grasp of decision diagrams, any manager can estimate the true value of information. Let's take a look at a disguised example we'll call Ace Grocery.

1. Do nothing

Todd Green, Ace's owner, was deeply concerned when a new competitor entered his area. A newspaper poll indicated that 20% of his customers planned to switch. But a consultant said that 50% of the potential defectors could be retained if Ace offered each $100 in retention rewards. Unfortunately, spending the $100 on loyal customers would probably not make them more loyal, and Ace didn't know which customers were which. Todd began to sketch out his options.

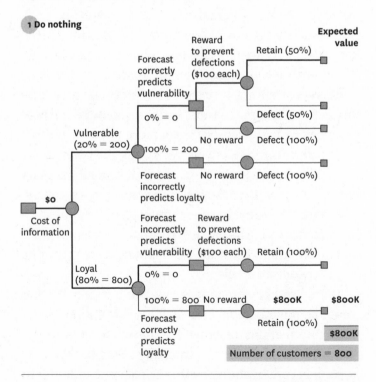

Ace had 1,000 customers, each worth an average of $1,000. If Todd did nothing, he'd retain only 80% of them, and Ace's value would fall from $1 million to $800,000. Todd tried another option.

2. Give $100 to everyone

Todd would lose fewer customers but would spend so much that the store's expected value would still fall to $800,000. Todd began to wonder if he could use CRM data to predict which customers would defect. He estimated how much that would be worth.

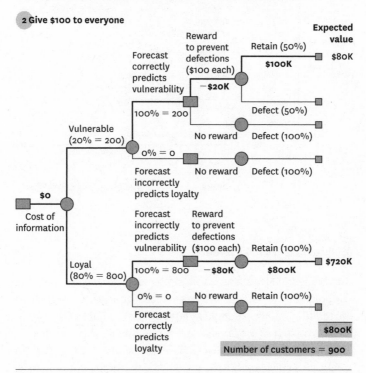

3. Reward just the right customers

If Todd could manage to offer $100 to all (and only) the potential defectors, Ace's expected value would only fall to $880,000. So $80,000 became the most Todd would pay for perfect information.

(continued)

Calculating the Cost of CRM (Continued)

3 Reward just the right customers

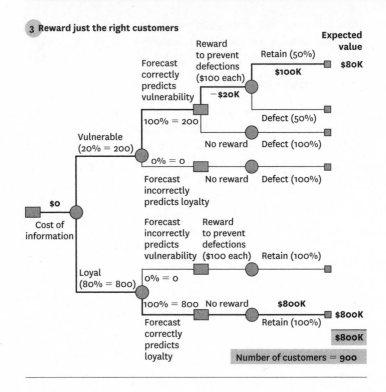

4. Purchase a CRM system

Todd called CRM Systems, a software vendor with the best package for predicting defectors. The system cost $20,000, but Todd estimated that additional implementation costs would add another $30,000. That $50,000 was still far below the $80,000 hurdle rate, so Todd asked for a meeting. He learned that the CRM system could correctly identify 60% of potential defectors. Unfortunately, 30% of loyal customers would also be identified as potential defectors. Todd calculated the value of this "imperfect" information.

Since the implementation of this software would drop Ace's value to $774,000, Todd rejected the proposal. Todd decided that the best approach was to offer all customers $100. Ace would retain

900 customers instead of 800, and his most loyal customers would not feel shortchanged.

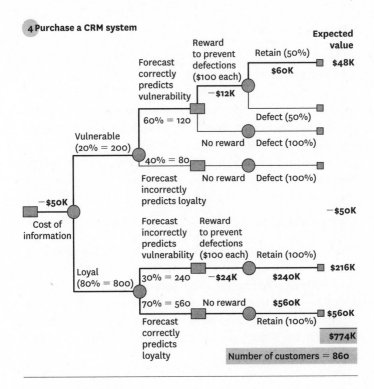

4 Purchase a CRM system

What Todd Learned

Through this process, Todd learned to address four critical questions.

How good is the information?

Todd knew that the value of information generally rises with its immediacy (making timely actions possible) and accuracy (making actions more productive). But Todd learned that reported accuracy often tells only half the story. Correctly predicting 60% of defectors sounded good until Todd's analysis showed that 30% of the loyal 80% would also be wrongly labeled as potential defectors.

(continued)

Calculating the Cost of CRM (Continued)

That would mean that a customer identified as a potential defector would be a true defector only 33% of the time. Forecasting is not always more valuable than guessing.

What is it good for?

Information that helps satisfy customers is far more valuable than information that merely satisfies curiosity. Todd calculated that the imperfect CRM information combined with a $100 retention program that saved only 50% of vulnerable customers created an expected value of just $774,000. However, if the $100 retention program could save 100% of vulnerable customers, the same CRM system would create an expected value of $834,000. Of course, offering loyalty rewards to every customer would now create an even greater value—$900,000.

What are the costs?

Todd's analysis demonstrated that the $20,000 CRM costs were swamped by the additional expenses of training, data collection, data analysis, information dissemination, and implementation programs. If Ace had failed to include these costs, it would have incorrectly calculated an expected value of $804,000, chosen to implement the system, and actually destroyed value.

Which results matter most?

Although expected values were necessary, they weren't sufficient for the final decision. Several other considerations, including the number of retained customers and fairness to loyal patrons, proved crucial as Todd weighed Ace's options.

September 2001 and then adding centers at two- to four-week intervals. This staggered approach allowed Brother to refine the system as it was implemented and adjust the training program as circumstances warranted.

The results have been impressive. The system can identify customers as they call in, quickly locate their purchase records, and supply call center workers with standard responses to common questions. That's reduced individual call times by 43 seconds on average, resulting in substantial savings. Brother estimates, for example, that this year the total savings could reach $635,000. What's more, Brother is now answering an average of 140,000 calls a month, and the typical customer is left on hold for less than five minutes. The newly automated process has also cut the time required to train new call center operators, saving even more money. Product returns fell by a third, from 5.0% in fiscal 2000 to 3.4% the following year.

And the benefits reach beyond the call centers. Because the system can capture data on the nature of incoming calls, it has given the company important new insights into customers' needs and behavior. That has improved Brother's ability to tailor outreach campaigns, which include surveys and newsletters, to well-defined buyer segments. Now that it has better information on the questions most frequently asked about its products, the company can use its campaigns to disseminate answers in advance. That, in turn, has reduced the volume of inquiries coming into the call centers. Each day, Brother sends data on types of inquiries and customer problems from the call centers to its corporate parent in Japan, where the information collected helps the company's product-planning, design, and customer-satisfaction groups evaluate both product performance and customers' preferences and experiences. Brother expects the exchange will lead to improved customer satisfaction and enhanced product performance over time.

Used the right way, real-time information can help companies cope with high levels of complexity in their customer relationship cycle, making priorities clear. Molex, an Illinois-based global manufacturer of electronic and fiber-optic interconnection systems, has a large customer base and a vast pipeline of potential orders. At any given moment, the company is pursuing close to 15,000 different sales opportunities worldwide. For years, Molex used e-mail and spreadsheets to keep track of its pipeline, but the resulting data were often weeks out of date. That made it difficult to consistently set sales priorities so the company could pursue the leads with the highest potential. The lack of updated information also made it hard to synchronize Molex's global efforts. Because the firm had so many major customers with operations in different parts of the world, several Molex locations could be working on similar or related programs for the same customer without knowing it.

In 2002, therefore, the company installed a CRM system to manage its order pipeline. For the first time, executives from the CEO on down could see the full range of sales opportunities in real time. That made it possible to measure the real value of those opportunities and get updated information about them 24 hours a day, rather than just a few times a year.

The gains were immediate: improved order management, more precise sales targets, and better global coordination of inventory and pricing between regions. Since implementation, both the number and the value of potential sales in the pipeline have climbed significantly, as the sales staff has used the shared information to identify opportunities earlier. Molex's management believes it is meeting the original goal of the project, which was a 5% increase in revenues.

Once the initial implementation was complete, moreover, management realized that the data being captured could also be used to improve budget planning. The pipeline data now form the foundation of the revenue portion of the budget process, and the company plans to use the information for parts forecasting and supply chain management as well.

Where Do We Go From Here?

As Kimberly-Clark, Brother, and Molex found, the data produced by a narrowly focused CRM system often reveal additional opportunities for important business refinements. And those refinements, taken together, can amount to a broad CRM application that extends across the company. The difference between this sort of wide-ranging CRM implementation and the prerecession CRM applications is that each step in building the system represents a carefully planned, well-defined advancement in strategic thinking. Kimberly-Clark started with trade promotion management then extended its tool set to include total retailer customer management and, more recently, consumer management. Brother's call centers have enhanced its U.S. marketing and outreach campaigns and even fed its product development and quality control processes on the other side of the world. Molex's clear view into its order pipeline has led to improvements in budgeting, procurement, and supply chain management.

Smart CRM adopters don't rest on their laurels. They rigorously analyze the data their systems produce to identify new, well-defined opportunities to extend the technology's power. In most cases, these opportunities lie in activities adjacent to the customer relationship cycle, as the natural path of these companies' CRM expansions show.

Aviall, for its part, plans to extend its CRM system in two directions—adding upstream links to its suppliers and downstream connections to its customers. These will give the firm an end-to-end view of the aviation supply chain, starting with the status of suppliers' inventory and extending all the way to customers' requirements for parts and maintenance. Because it will enable the firm to better match supply and demand, Aviall expects the expanded system to become an important source of competitive advantage.

It's also often possible to extend the benefits of CRM to related business units. Ingersoll-Rand, for example, recognized that the customers of its Club Car division— golf courses—were also potential buyers of its other divisions' products, such as Bobcat miniexcavators and loaders. Extending its CRM system to include those divisions could create new opportunities for cross selling. The company began to do just that in late 2002, and already the number of new leads generated has been substantial—an additional $6.2 million worth of leads for other Ingersoll-Rand products in the first year. That success has led to even broader plans.

Today, Ingersoll-Rand wants to use CRM as the glue to bind together all four of its operating sectors (which represent more than 100 worldwide manufacturing facilities) so that the company can operate as one integrated enterprise in the eyes of its customers. Like Aviall, Ingersoll-Rand may utterly transform its business through its investments in CRM, but again the changes will come in carefully measured stages, with success building on success.

Business Before Technology

You'll have noticed that we haven't spent a lot of time describing the details of the technology in this article. That's intentional. In evaluating and designing CRM systems, business needs should take precedence over technological capabilities. Managers should not be distracted by what CRM software *can* do; they should concentrate instead on what it *should* do—both for their companies and for their customers (see the sidebar, "McDonald's Tech Turnaround"). Fortunately, as competition among CRM vendors is increasing the software is rapidly becoming more flexible. It's not yet simple to install a CRM system, but the technology is getting more dependable, the implementation process is becoming more streamlined, and the failure rate is going down.

That gives companies the freedom to apply CRM with greater precision, targeting critical gaps in their

McDonald's Tech Turnaround

IT WAS NOTHING IF not ambitious. In January 2001, fast-food giant McDonald's launched a five-year, $1 billion initiative to overhaul its information systems to enhance customer service at its more than 30,000 restaurants around the world. The vast effort, dubbed "Innovate," involved installing a new, Internet-based data management infrastructure for the company that would cover everything from electronic links with suppliers to software for tracking customer purchasing patterns to sensors for remotely monitoring the temperature of fat in french-fry vats. The company believed that once the new systems were in place, it would be able to scrutinize every detail of its business in real time, ensuring that each outlet fine-tuned its operation to serve customers flawlessly.

But just two years after Innovate's launch, a new CEO, Jim Cantalupo, pulled the plug on the project, announcing that McDonald's would take a $170 million write-off related to the termination of the initiative. Facing financial pressures and an eroding stock price, Cantalupo (who died suddenly a year later in April 2004) determined that, to revitalize itself, McDonald's needed to focus on two priorities: customers and existing restaurants. The massive IT program simply would not deliver enough improvements in those areas to justify the enormous expense and operational disruptions it presented.

McDonald's might be an extreme example—billion-dollar IT initiatives remain rare—but it also offers encouraging news. After disbanding the Innovate initiative, the company launched a series of more modest CRM efforts—such as installing touch screen–ordering systems and improving a customer service hotline—aimed at solving particular customer relationship problems. These highly targeted efforts have contributed to a resurgence in sales and profits.

customer relationship cycles where performance suffers. By setting priorities for their information requirements carefully, making sure they're guided by overall customer strategy, companies can launch highly disciplined CRM efforts that will have a greater impact with lower investment and less risk. CRM, in other words, is coming to resemble any other valuable management tool, and the keys to successful implementation are also becoming familiar: strong executive and business-unit leadership, careful strategic planning, clear performance measures, and a coordinated program that combines organizational and process changes with the application of new technology. No longer a black hole, CRM is becoming a basic building block of corporate success.

DARRELL K. RIGBY is a partner with Bain & Company and directs the firm's Global Retail practice. **DIANNE LEDINGHAM** is a partner and leader in Bain's Technology and Performance Improvement practices.

Originally published in November 2004. Reprint R0411H

Diamonds in the Data Mine

by Gary Loveman

IT'S A FRIDAY NIGHT ON the Las Vegas Strip, and all of the neighbors are making spectacles of themselves. The $750 million Mirage boasts a Vesuvian volcano that erupts loudly every 15 minutes. Next door, at Treasure Island, a faux British frigate battles a pirate ship at regular intervals. Further down the Strip, the Bellagio sports a lake festooned with sparkling, dancing fountains that beckon to passing tourists.

Meanwhile, the customer pulling into Harrah's Las Vegas is dazzled more by the service than the building. A smiling valet greets her by name. Instead of having to wade through a crowded lobby to reach the casino, she steps quickly into the gaming room and sits down at a slot machine. The card reader on the machine pages her host, who approaches every so often to ensure that she's happy with the service she's receiving. Although the customer doesn't fit the stereotypical profile of a Las Vegas high roller, Harrah's makes sure she feels special. Because the casino delivers the recognition and service she has come to expect, she'll return to Harrah's again and again.

Harrah's Entertainment has the most devoted clientele in the casino industry—a business notorious for fickle customers. That loyalty to Harrah's, which now operates 26 casinos in 13 states, has enabled the gaming company to record 16 straight quarters of same-store revenue growth. In 2002, Harrah's posted more than $4 billion in revenue and $235 million in net income.

We've increased customer loyalty, even in the current challenging economy, in two ways. First, we use database marketing and decision-science-based analytical tools to widen the gap between us and casino operators who base their customer incentives more on intuition than evidence. Second, we deliver the great service that consumers demand. In short, we've come out on top in the casino wars by mining our customer data deeply, running marketing experiments, and using the results to develop and implement finely tuned marketing and service-delivery strategies that keep our customers coming back.

A Dicey Business

By the time I had left Harvard Business School to join the corporation as chief operating officer in 1998, Harrah's had become the first nationwide casino business, thanks to a geographic diversification plan promulgated by Phil Satre, the company's chairman and then-chief executive officer. Satre led the wave of gaming growth in the 1990s, expanding Harrah's from

Idea in Brief

In an industry notorious for fickle customers, Harrah's Entertainment has the most devoted clientele. It's recorded 16 straight quarters of revenue growth in its 26 casinos. In economically sluggish 2002, it posted $4 billion+ in revenues—while rivals wilted.

Harrah's secret? Not billion-dollar facilities boasting fiery volcanoes and sparkling fountains. Instead, its employees dazzle customers with exceptional service. Valets greet them by name, hosts ensure they're happy, and the company rewards them handsomely for choosing Harrah's.

To develop its marketing and service-delivery strategies, Harrah's doesn't rely on intuition or assume that "if you build it, they will come." Rather, it uses sophisticated, proprietary technology to deeply mine its customer database. By slicing information into ever-finer segments, Harrah's gets to know its customers better and better. It continually enhances the benefits of choosing its casinos over flashier rivals.

four casinos in two states to 26 casinos across 13 states currently.

Satre's vision differed markedly from the strategy pursued by other big casino operators, whose "If you build it, they will come" philosophy focused on attracting customers to a fantasyland Las Vegas. Companies such as Mandalay Resort Group and MGM–Mirage invested heavily in constructing costly must-see casinos offering a wide range of amenities—fabulous spas, high-end shopping malls, dazzling shows—designed to appeal to a broader audience than simply gamblers. Their hope was that such facilities would attract an ever-growing number of new customers. This strategy ultimately transformed both the Las Vegas skyline and tourist spending patterns: The Las Vegas Convention and Visitors Authority reported that, in 2001, revenues

Idea in Practice

How to use your database to secure customers' loyalty? Consider Harrah's approach:

1. Acquire a rich repository of customer information.

Example: Total Gold customers inserted cards into slot machines and earned rewards for playing while Harrah's gathered information about them. A transactional database recorded each customer's activity at various points of sale—slot machines, restaurants, retail areas—at all Harrah's properties, not just one casino. Harrah's fed that information into its enterprise data warehouse, which contained data on customer demographics, spending, and preferences.

2. Slice and dice data finely to develop marketing strategies.

Most companies do the opposite: design grand marketing schemes, then adjust their databases to those strategies.

Example: Harrah's database information indicated the need for a loyalty strategy that would motivate customers to visit Harrah's casinos more regularly—just as they routinely visit their hairdressers or mechanics. How? By enveloping customers in *reasons* to be loyal—cultivating intimately friendly relationships with them.

3. Identify core customers by predicting their lifetime value.

Instead of emphasizing how much people spent during one transaction, calculate their potential worth *over time*.

Example: Harrah's discovered 26% of its gamblers generated 82% of its revenue. And top customers weren't high rollers—but

from dining, entertainment, shopping, and other activities outpaced the city's casino revenues by a three-to-one margin.

Satre, by contrast, focused on expanding the corporation's gaming business outside Nevada and Atlantic City, seeing geographic diversification as an opportunity to introduce the Harrah's brand to new customers and to middle-aged and senior adults with discretionary time and income. Because they enjoyed playing slots, they welcomed free casino chips more than rooms or dinners as rewards. Very happy customers spent 24% more annually; disappointed customers spent 10% less.

4. Gather increasingly specific information about customers' preferences—then *appeal* to those interests.

Reward customers for spending more, which increases their lifetime value.

> *Example:* Harrah's split Total Rewards cardholding customers into tiers based on their annual theoretical value, and treated the groups differently. For example, "Gold" customers waited in lines at reception desks or restaurants; "Platinum" customers waited in

shorter lines; "Diamond" customers rarely waited. Seeing the perks others had, customers spent more to earn the higher-tier cards.

5. Reward employees for prioritizing customer service.

> *Example:* Harrah's measures employees' speed and friendliness, paying bonuses for improving customer-satisfaction scores. Rewards hinge on *everyone's* performance at a casino—and on customer satisfaction, not a property's financial performance. In 2002, Harrah's paid nonmanagement workers $14.2 million in bonuses.

insulate the company from regional economic vagaries. Once Harrah's posted high returns in these emerging markets, its competitors also began to expand into them. But Satre believed that competing largely on the basis of billion-dollar facilities in the face of new competition was not the most prudent use of capital because the returns on such buildings often weaken when the novelty wanes.

Fortunately, Satre had two important arrows in his quiver. First, he knew that, unlike its competitors, Harrah's didn't depend heavily on its stores, restaurants, bars, or shows; it drew the lion's share of its revenues—87.2% in 2001—from its casinos. He also suspected that cultivating lasting relationships with the company's core customers—slot players—would lead to greater and more sustainable profit growth. So he opted to invest in development of the intellectual and technological capabilities needed to assemble and analyze data about those customers. The goal was to provide good service to them and thus encourage their loyalty to the company's brand. When Satre hired me as COO, he said he wanted to change Harrah's from an operations-driven company that viewed each casino as a stand-alone business into a marketing-driven company that built customer loyalty to all Harrah's properties.

One tactic the company had already decided to use to enhance customer loyalty was called Total Gold, a player-card program that was modeled after the airline industry's frequent-flier programs. Launched in 1997, Total Gold was designed to provide regular customers with incentives to visit Harrah's properties throughout the country. Customers inserted their Total Gold cards into slot machines and earned credits as they played. They were rewarded with the standard fare that all casinos offer—free hotel rooms, dinners, show tickets, gift certificates. But there were three problems with the program. First, nothing differentiated this program from our competitors' efforts. Our customers simply took their free rooms and dinners and drifted across the street to do their gambling. Second, our customers earned different rewards at different properties; there was no uniformity in the program. Third, and most important, our customers were not given any incentives to consolidate their gaming with Harrah's.

While Total Gold wasn't much good for keeping customers loyal to Harrah's, it was quietly digging our future diamond mine. By tracking millions of individual transactions, the information-technology systems that underlie the program had assembled a vast amount of data on customer preferences. At the core of the Total Gold rewards program (and its successor, Total Rewards, which I'll describe below) was a 300-gigabyte transactional database that recorded customer activity at various points of sale—slot machines, restaurants, and other retail areas in our properties. Database managers fed that information into our enterprise data warehouse, which contained not only millions of transactional data points about customers (such as names, addresses, ages, genders) but also details about their gambling spending and preferences. The database was a very rich repository of customer information.

Slicing the Dicing

When we started digging into the database, one statistic stood out: Our Total Gold cardholders told us in surveys and focus groups that they were spending only 36% of their annual gaming budgets at Harrah's. This presented an opportunity. There was a promise of tremendous upside if we could induce customers to spend more of their gaming money at Harrah's *and* if we could communicate effectively with them. I suggested to Satre that we might be able to divert more of our customers' annual gaming budgets to Harrah's if we borrowed a page from the playbooks of other businesses whose case studies I'd long taught. Basically, we needed to do what the Starbucks and Nordstroms of the world had done—change the way consumers made decisions about our merchandise.

To do that, we clearly needed to slice and dice the data finely enough that we could develop effective marketing programs. Common practice calls for defining marketing strategies apart from database strategies— that is, the company comes up with a grand marketing scheme and then tries to adjust the database to its strategies. Unlike many companies, we decided to let the data suggest the specific marketing ideas to us.

The information we found in our database indicated that a loyalty strategy based on same-store sales growth would work. Same-store sales is a classic measurement of a simple retail-loyalty strategy: The goal is to get a customer to visit your store regularly, just as she might routinely visit her hairdresser and mechanic. The hairdresser and the mechanic envelop the client in reasons to be loyal, primarily by developing a friendly relationship. We decided to develop just this kind of close relationship with the people who visit Harrah's casinos.

Before we could persuade customers to come back time after time, however, we needed to take a hard look at them and understand how much value each of them brought to us. We discovered that 26% of the gamblers who visited Harrah's generated 82% of our revenues.

We were surprised to find out who our best customers really were. They emphatically were *not* the gold cuff-linked, limousine-riding high rollers we and our competitors had fawned over for many years. Instead, they turned out to be former teachers, doctors, bankers, and machinists—middle-aged and senior adults with discretionary time and income who enjoyed playing slot machines.

We also learned that these customers typically did not stay in a hotel but visited a casino on the way home from work or on a weekend night out. At the same time, we found that our target customers often responded better to an offer of $60 of casino chips than to a free room, two steak meals, and $30 worth of chips because they enjoyed the anticipation and excitement of gambling itself. And we were able to develop quantitative models that allowed us to predict, based on an individual's play, his or her "customer worth"—the theoretical amount we could expect the customer to spend not just during one evening but over the long term.

Suddenly, we saw how we could differentiate our brand. Understanding the lifetime value of our customers would be critical to our marketing strategy. Instead of focusing on how much people spent in our casinos during a single visit, it became clear that we needed to focus on their potential worth over time. For instance, we could see that customers who said they were very happy with the Harrah's experience increased their spending on gambling at Harrah's by 24% per year; customers who said they were disappointed with Harrah's decreased their spending by 10% per year.

The best way to engage in this kind of data-driven marketing is to gather more and more specific information about customer preferences, run experiments and analyses on the new data, and determine ways of appealing to players' interests. We realized that the information in our database, coupled with decision-science tools that enabled us to predict individual customers' theoretical value to us, would allow us to create marketing interventions that profitably addressed players' unique preferences. The more we appealed to these preferences, the more money the customers would spend with us.

So we decided to act on a radical idea: We would reward customers for spending in ways that added to their value. Most consumer businesses insist that they can't treat one customer differently than they treat another, even though some customers are obviously worth much more than others. To us, that approach was fundamentally wrong, but it didn't mean that we had to focus on the relatively small number of high rollers. Rather, we made a point of treating our millions of regular customers differently depending on their value to us.

It turned out that our customers—I would venture to say all customers—actually enjoy aspiring to higher levels of achievement and reward. It's simply human nature. Understanding this, we split our customers into three tiers: Gold, Platinum, and Diamond cardholders, based on their annual theoretical value. Platinum and Diamond cardholders receive greater levels of service, which adds an aspirational element to the program. For example, our database told us that our best customers wanted service quickly—they didn't want to wait in line to park their cars, or eat in restaurants, or check in at the front desk. So we decided to make a point of routing our customers into three different lines. People who weren't card-carrying Harrah's members and Gold customers stood in lines at the reception desk or the restaurant. Platinum customers would stand in still shorter lines, and Diamond cardholders would rarely ever have to stand in line. This created a visible differentiation in customer service.

It was essential for our customers to see the perks that others were getting. Once we divided the lines this way, we watched as our customers did what they could to earn the higher-tiered cards. Every experience in our casino was redesigned to drive customers to want to earn a higher-level card. As it turns out, marketing that appeals to customer aspiration works wonderfully.

We also set up a series of triggers in the database and analyzed the customers' responses to those triggers. If, for example, we discovered that a customer who spends $1,000 per month with us hadn't visited us in three months, a letter or telephone call would invite him back. If we learned that he lost money during his last visit, we invited him back for a special event. Our telemarketers were trained to listen for responses to specific offers—a certain percentage of our customers responded positively to offers of a steak dinner; others would respond to offers of two free nights in the hotel.

Once entered into our database, these responses provided fodder for more slicing, dicing, and experimentation. It's important to note that our database strategy hinged on our ability to combine data from all of our properties, so customers could use their reward cards in multiple locations. Combining transactional data from all our sites was so important that we developed and ultimately patented the technology to do it.

We also decided to use our transactional data to "sell" our slot machines. In the past, we had no way of knowing why customers chose to play at certain machines. Was it because of the way the machines looked? Or because other machines were occupied? Or was it because we had signs on top of them proclaiming the odds? Our transactional database told us exactly what the patterns of play were in our casinos. We discovered that at any given time, it was possible to know which specific customers were playing at particular slots in Harrah's Las Vegas and what it was about that specific machine that appealed to them. This knowledge allowed us to configure the casino floor with a mix of slot machines that benefited both our customers and our company.

Hitting the Customer Service Jackpot

Deep data mining and decision-science marketing would be worth little in driving same-store sales growth were it not for another simultaneously applied and extremely critical ingredient—an absolute focus on customer satisfaction. When I came to the casino business, there was an insufficient focus on customer service. We decided that great service would allow us to build—just as Home Depot, Four Seasons, and other great brands do in their fields—the capacity to brand ourselves as the only nationwide consumer gaming business.

Customer service is something most organizations say they focus on. But, in fact, they often fail to institute systems to use customer service to reinforce loyalty with carrots and sticks. Our data told us that our customers want friendly and helpful attention in addition to fast service. We decided to link employee rewards to customer satisfaction. Accordingly, we chose to measure all employee performance on the matrices of speed and friendliness. The better the experience the guest had, the more money employees stood to make. To this end, all Harrah's employees take part in a certification program that trains them to deliver excellent service. From housekeepers to slot attendants, from valets to stewards, from receptionists to chefs, all employees are told daily as they arrive at work: If your service can persuade one customer to make one more visit a year with us, you've had a good shift. If you can persuade three, you've had a great shift.

We implemented a bonus plan to reward hourly workers with extra cash for achieving improved customer satisfaction scores, which we culled from very detailed customer surveys. If a property's overall rating rose 3% or more, each employee could earn $75 to $200. What has made the bonus program work is that the reward depends on everyone's performance. If the valet's scores were low but the steak house receptionist's were high, the receptionist would check in on the valet. Likewise, if one property received low scores and another high ones, the general manager of the lower-scoring property might visit his colleague to find out what he could do to improve his property's scores.

It's important to note that we chose to measure customer satisfaction scores independent of a property's financial performance. In 2002, one property had record-breaking financial results, but employees did not receive bonuses because their customer service scores were mediocre. Our employees are obsessed with their property's customer satisfaction scores for a good reason: In 2002, we paid $14.2 million in bonuses to nonmanagement employees based on their properties' customer satisfaction scores. Since the program's inception, Harrah's has paid out more than $43 million in bonuses.

This score-driven customer satisfaction measure has allowed properties—even those in troubled markets—to continue to grow. Take, for example, our casino in Laughlin, Nevada. Despite strong competition and a mere 1% increase in the local market's gaming revenues in 2002, Harrah's Laughlin recorded a 14% gain in revenues. Why? Because its customers were loyal, thanks to great service. In fact, the employees at Harrah's Laughlin earned the highest customer service scores in the company.

Our experience with customer service has shown us that meeting budget at the expense of service is a very bad idea. If you're not making your numbers, you don't cut back on staff. In fact, just the reverse: The better the experience a guest has and the more attentive you are to him, the more money you'll make. For Harrah's, good customer service is not a matter of an isolated incident or two but of daily routine. When he goes off duty, the Laughlin general manager tells employees to call him at home—anytime, day or night—whenever they see five people waiting in any line. To us, this is living proof that our same-store sales growth in tough markets has been driven by sustained attention to great customer service.

The Winning Hand

Everything we do to market Harrah's is framed in terms of players' decisions to visit, or not visit, one of our casinos. One measure of the effectiveness of our strategy is that many of our competitors have adopted similar programs after viewing our company's performance over the past few years. But our competitors continue to focus largely on facilities, while we keep combining improved facilities with breakthroughs in marketing and customer service. We maintain our competitive advantage by using our human capital and technology systems to get to know our customers better.

Harrah's will keep adding excitement and benefits to the Total Rewards program, widening its scope across gaming-related activities. And we'll keep enhancing the benefits that players get from consolidating their gaming within our brands.

Let the neighbors lure tourists with knights on horseback, fiery volcanoes, pirate ships, and mini-Manhattans. We'll just keep refining what we're already pretty good at: drilling into our data and making sure our regular customers are more than satisfied.

GARY LOVEMAN is the CEO of Harrah's Entertainment and a former Harvard Business School professor.

Originally published in May 2003. Reprint R0305H

Want to Perfect Your Company's Service?

Use Behavioral Science

by Richard B. Chase and Sriram Dasu

WHAT DON'T WE KNOW ABOUT service management? For the past 15 years, legions of scholars and practitioners have studied the subject. They've applied queuing theory to bank lines. They've deified well-run call centers. They've measured response times to the tenth decimal point. They've built cults around "moments of truth," "service recovery," and "delighting the customer."

It may appear, then, that no stone in the service-management garden has been left unturned, not to mention analyzed, polished, and replaced. Surprisingly little time, however, has been spent examining service encounters from the customer's point of view. Specifically, practitioners haven't carefully considered the underlying psychology of service encounters—the feelings that customers experience during these encounters, feelings so subtle they probably couldn't be put into words.

Fortunately, behavioral science offers new insights into better service management. For decades, behavioral and cognitive scientists have studied how people experience social interactions, form judgments, and store memories—as well as what biases they bring to bear on daily life. Their findings hold important lessons for the executives who design and manage service encounters. First, the research tells us a lot about how customers experience the passage of time: when time seems to drag, when it speeds by, and when in a sequence of events an uncomfortable experience will be least noticeable. Second, it helps us understand how customers interpret an event after it's over. For example, people seem to be hardwired to blame an individual rather than a poorly designed system when something goes wrong.

In this article, we'll translate findings from behavioral-science research into operating principles for service-encounter management. And we'll show how managers can optimize those extraordinarily important moments when the company touches its customers—for better and for worse.

Applied Behavioral Science

In any service encounter—from a simple pizza pickup to a complex, long-term consulting engagement—perception is reality. That is, what really matters is how the customer interprets the encounter. Behavioral science can shed light on the complex processes involved in the formation of those perceptions. In particular, it

Idea in Brief

It may seem like the topic of service management has been exhausted. Legions of scholars and practitioners have applied queuing theory to bank lines, measured response times to the millisecond, and created cults around "delighting the customer." But practitioners haven't carefully considered the underlying psychology of service encounters—the feelings that customers experience during these encounters, feelings often so subtle they probably couldn't be put into words. Fortunately, behavioral science offers new insights into better service management. In this article, the authors translate findings from behavioral-science research into five operating principles: 1) finish strong; 2) get the bad experiences out of the way early; 3) segment the pleasure, combine the pain; 4) build commitment through choice; and 5) give people rituals and stick to them. Ultimately, only one thing really matters in a service encounter—the customer's perception of what occurred. This article will help you engineer your service encounters to enhance your customers' experiences during the process as well as their recollections of the process after it is completed.

can help managers understand how people react to the sequence and duration of events, and how they rationalize experiences after they occur.

Sequence Effects

According to behavioral scientists, when people recall an experience, they don't remember every single moment of it (unless the experience was short and traumatic). Instead, they recall a few significant moments vividly and gloss over the others—they remember snapshots, not movies. And they carry away an overall assessment of the experience that's based on three factors: the trend in the sequence of pain or pleasure, the high and low points, and the ending.

End on an Uptick

DANIEL KAHNEMAN, a professor of psychology at Princeton University, is a leading researcher in cognitive psychology. In a 1993 experiment, he and his colleagues asked subjects to choose between two unpleasant experiences. In the first, subjects immersed their hands in uncomfortably cool water (57° F) for 60 seconds. In the second, the same subjects immersed their hand in cool water (57° F) for 60 seconds followed by 30 seconds in slightly warmer water (59° F). Even though the second sequence extended the total discomfort time, when subjects were asked which experience they would repeat, nearly 70% chose the second one.

Kahneman found similar results in a field experiment he performed with D.A. Redelmeier. They learned that prolonging a colonoscopy by leaving the colonoscope in place for about a minute after the procedure was completed—thus decreasing the level of discomfort for the final moments of the procedure—produced significant improvements in patients' perceptions of the experience.

Not surprisingly, people prefer a sequence of experiences that improve over time. When gambling, they prefer to lose $10 first, then win $5, rather than win $5, then lose $10. There is also evidence that people pay attention to the rate of improvement in a sequence—clearly preferring ones that improve faster. And, most intriguing, the ending matters enormously. (See the sidebar "End on an Uptick.") A terrible ending usually dominates a person's recollection of an experience.

Duration Effects
Psychologists and cognitive scientists have poured enormous effort into unraveling the mysteries of how

people process time. When do they pay attention to the passage of time, and how do they estimate its duration? Although much of the mystery still remains, one finding that's been verified repeatedly is that people who are mentally engaged in a task don't notice how long it takes. Another is that, when prompted to pay attention to the passage of time, people overestimate the time elapsed. A third finding is that increasing the number of segments in an encounter lengthens its perceived duration. For example, a ten-minute dance sequence consisting of four segments will seem longer than one identical in length but split into two segments.

Since perceptions of time's passage are so subjective, the obvious question is, When does duration matter? Research indicates that unless an activity is much longer or much shorter than expected, people pay little attention to its duration. There are two reasons for this. First, the pleasurable content of the experience and how it is arranged—rather than how long it takes—seem to dominate people's assessments. And second, aside from one-off transactions such as buying a cup of coffee, service encounters are rarely identical in length, so people have only general reference points for evaluating duration. Their estimates of how long it will take to visit a tax accountant—or go to a ball game, or have minor surgery—are likely to be fuzzy.

Rationalization Effects

People desperately want things to make sense; if there's no handy explanation for an unexpected event,

Why cruises work

Modern cruise lines apply many of the operating principles suggested by behavioral science.

Principle	What cruise lines do
Finish strong	End each day on a high note with raffles, contests, shows, and so on.
	End the cruise with the captain's dinner.
	Pass out keepsakes or bottles of wine upon reaching home port.
Segment the pleasure	Pack many events into one short vacation.
Create rituals	Offer captain's dinner and midnight buffets.

they'll concoct one. Behavioral scientists call this "counterfactual thinking," but it's simpler to call it second-guessing.

People second-guess because they want one clear reason for why something happened. In their mental simulation, they try to capture the specific what-ifs: "If only *x* hadn't happened, things would be different." Three characteristics stand out in this simulation. First, they view the likely cause as a discrete thing, not a continuous, intertwined process. For example, people are more likely to blame a missed plane on "the backup in the tunnel" than on a cluster of events that—in conjunction—caused their late arrival. Second, people often conclude that deviations from rituals and norms caused the unexpected outcome. Professional sports are loaded with players who follow rituals religiously: some baseball players avoid stepping on the foul line at all costs, and many basketball players have particular dribbling routines before shooting a free throw. Third, people tend to ascribe credit or blame to individuals, not systems. Even when they clearly see that the computer system caused the hotel bill error, for example, they tend to blame the clerk. They want to put a human face on the problem. One final note about ascribing blame: people are far less apt to "search for the guilty" if they think they've had some control over the process that occurred. The more empowered and engaged they feel, the less angry they are when something goes wrong.

In summary, people want explanations, and they'll make them up if they have to. The explanation will nearly always focus on something they can observe—something that is discrete and concrete enough to be changed in their if-only fantasies.

Several operating principles for service-encounter management emerge from the behavioral-science findings we've just reviewed.

Principle 1: Finish Strong

Most service providers believe that the beginning and end of an encounter—the so-called service bookends—are equally weighted in the eyes of the customer. They're dead wrong. The end is far more important because it's what remains in the customer's recollections. Sure, it's important to achieve a base level of satisfactory performance at the beginning, but a company is better off with a relatively weak start and a modest upswing at the end than with a boffo start and a so-so ending.

People's innate preference for improvement is another factor in this principle. We believe that the desire for improvement applies not only to lengthy encounters but also to short, technology-mediated encounters, such as on a Web site. The fact is, very few Web designers have thought this issue through. Most companies spare no expense to make their home pages attractive; a great deal of thought goes into questions of aesthetics, content, and navigation in the top page or two. This is an eminently logical strategy, given the need to get people to enter and engage with the site. However, too many Web encounters start strong then go downhill fast. Our cursory review of commercial Web sites uncovered an alarming number of problems: difficulty in exiting the site if an item is out of stock; difficulty in canceling an order if the shipping charges are too high; no notification of security for credit card information, and so on. Make no mistake, the frustrated customer remembers the messy final experience far more clearly than the jazzy, supposedly sticky home page.

That which applies to short encounters goes double for longer service encounters like consulting projects. While it often makes sense to pick low-hanging fruit at the outset, a consultant would be well advised (other things being equal) to schedule the project so that a golden nugget or two appear at the end of the engagement. For instance, a consultant that's hired to reengineer a company's business processes might start with the distribution center and move to the call center later in the project, because he knows from past experience that the call center changes will likely reap a windfall of savings. What you don't want is to have the project results become less and less impressive, even if (as is often the case) its labor costs are following a staged decline. Even though one large consulting firm had performed admirably in its yearlong reengineering project, for example, it received low marks from its client. The consultants achieved more than the goals set, but the lack of a visible upswing in results at the end left the impression of mediocrity. As it turns out, last impressions—not first impressions—endure.

Compare that with another consulting project that ended quite naturally on a high note. A statistician colleague of ours was hired to determine what factors accounted for the sales success of a new video game. The client agreed at the start that the project would be a success if the consultant's model could explain just 6% of the variability in sales among a dozen competing video games. The consultant made progress over the first three months of the project, but it wasn't until the last day of the schedule that the analysis yielded a three-factor combination that explained more than 90% of the variability in sales. (For the gamers out there, these factors were kid testing, advertising, and the number of outlets they could get the game into.) This positive surprise had far more impact than it would have had at the outset, since the clients' longer-term involvement had sensitized them to the complexity of the task. Our colleague was lucky to deliver such a clear, better-than-anticipated result; he was luckier still to have done so at the eleventh hour.

Even if you can't end with a substantive bang, it's smart to finish with a stylistic flourish. Consider the airline industry, which suffers from high levels of customer dissatisfaction due to flight delays and cancellations, inadequate legroom, and lost luggage. Without a doubt, those failures have to be addressed. But we'd guess that airlines could make up some ground if they paid more attention to their customers' last encounter—baggage collection. Why not offer a new service—aides to help passengers in the baggage claim area? Simply having someone there would show concern for passengers.

Malaysian Airlines is one of the few carriers that understands that the encounter isn't over when the customer steps off the plane. Several years ago, an acquaintance was traveling by Malaysian Airlines with her nine-month-old son. Even after nine years, she fondly recalls the help that the flight attendants gave her with baggage collection and ground transportation. It cost the airline little to provide that end-of-encounter assistance—and it gained a loyal customer who's described that experience to fellow travelers dozens of times since. As simple as that example sounds, such small touches have a disproportionate effect on customers' recollections.

Principle 2: Get the Bad Experiences Out of the Way Early

Behavioral science tells us that, in a sequence of events involving good and bad outcomes, people prefer to have undesirable events come first—so they can avoid dread—and to have desirable events come at the end of a sequence—so they can savor them.

This principle has concrete, immediate implications for how health care professionals manage their encounters with patients. Imagine Danielle, a pediatric dental hygienist, who has almost finished cleaning Asher's teeth. Asher, a skittish six-year-old and a frequent visitor to the clinic, suffers from a mild form of gingivitis and has several cavities. Danielle accidentally scrapes a particularly sensitive spot, causing the boy momentary pain. She still needs to clean two more teeth, which she is sure are not as sensitive. She could either end the cleaning now and resume on the next visit, or she could complete it today. Continuing would subject Asher to more discomfort, although it would be significantly less than what he just felt. She is also wondering whether continuing (hence, increasing the total pain) will affect Asher's perception of the cleaning experience and his behavior on subsequent visits.

According to behavioral research, Danielle should finish the job. Asher will carry away a better memory. He will remember the treatment, of course, but also that the pain "wasn't so bad at the end." Danielle will have extended a painful experience, yet because the ending was slightly less painful, Asher's overall assessment of it will improve.

Most companies' services don't cause physical pain, obviously. And often the discomfort that's part of a service encounter occurs early naturally: the wait in line (unpleasant) comes before the meal or the theme park ride (pleasant). When that's not the case, it may be necessary to extend the encounter to soften the ending experience.

In professional services, the unpleasantness often comes in the form of bad news. Most people want bad news brought to their attention right away. Unfortunately, service providers are human just like the rest of us—they dread delivering bad news, so they delay it until the last possible moment. This is exactly the wrong thing to do. Get bad news, pain, discomfort, long waits in line, and other unpleasant things out of the way as soon as possible so they don't dominate the customer's recollection of the entire experience.

Principle 3: Segment the Pleasure, Combine the Pain

As we noted earlier, experiences seem longer when they are broken into segments. In addition, people have an asymmetric reaction to losses and gains. Compare winning $10 in one gamble with winning $5 twice. Most of us would prefer to win twice. What about losing $10 in one game as compared with losing $5 in each of two gambles? Here, most people prefer only one loss. That's why companies should break pleasant experiences into multiple stages and combine unpleasant ones into a single stage.

Not many businesses have grasped this notion. Health care facilities, for example, typically make patients wait at multiple points before they see the physician, but doing so makes the overall wait appear even longer. Clinics would do better to let patients spend more time in the waiting room so they don't have to endure a second, third, or fourth wait in the examining rooms.

Phone help-line menus are frustrating in a similar way. To reach the department that can resolve a problem, a customer must listen to instructions and press (or voice) a response. It often takes four or five such steps to get to the right place. Even if the actual time required to run through, say, four menu queries is less than to run through two, people recall four as taking longer. Service companies would do well to cut the number of steps it takes to reach the final destination, thereby reducing the perceived pain of waiting.

The best trade shows have grasped both halves of this principle. They combine as many of the boring paperwork steps as possible. The Internet World trade show, for example, lets attendees preregister over the Internet. When they arrive, they simply pick up a badge that's been programmed with personal data. The badges allow them to get information at any booth—attendees just swipe them through a reading device, thus avoiding an endless exchange of business cards and sign-in sheets. The things that attendees enjoy and come to see, such as product demos, are plentiful, and they're spread throughout the conference.

Disney's theme parks also understand both halves of the principle. They do a great job of distracting customers who are waiting in line, thus lessening their discomfort. And they make the rides really short, as well. That's done primarily so that more people can get on them, but this efficiency has the added benefit of segmenting the pleasure, which in turn creates the perception of a longer and richer day at the theme park. From the customer's point of view, two 90-second rides last longer than one three-minute ride.

Principle 4: Build Commitment Through Choice

A fascinating study found that blood donors perceived significantly less discomfort when they were allowed to select the arm from which the blood would be drawn.[1] The lesson is clear: people are happier and more comfortable when they believe they have some control over a process, particularly an uncomfortable one. Often the control handed over is largely symbolic (as in the choice of arm). In other cases, it's very real: the medical profession has long recognized the value of allowing the patient to make an informed choice about alternative treatments for cancer and heart disease. These are extremely important, high-stakes decisions, and great value is gained by including the patient in the decision. He or she feels less helpless, less hopeless, and more committed to making the process work.

Many companies have learned to apply this principle in less life-threatening situations. Several airlines, for example, let passengers choose when they want to have their meal served during long flights. Most hotels give customers a choice of using an alarm clock or receiving a wake-up call. And some banks have moved away from snake line configurations and back to individual lines so that customers can work with their favorite teller.

As one Midwestern company learned, this principle can both save money and make clients happy. Customers were complaining to the Xerox machine-servicing company that repairs didn't happen quickly enough. At first, the company considered adding more repair personnel, but upon reflection, it decided to give customers more choice over the schedule. It let them determine the urgency of the problem—service people would arrive faster for a critical failure than for a less urgent one. As expected, this improved customer satisfaction, but what surprised the company was that fewer repair people were needed. The change also reduced the turnover of customer service reps because there were fewer scheduling conflicts with the customers. Conventional wisdom would say that allowing customers to pick the time would force the company to hire more staff. Here, however, as is often the case, customers actually wanted choice more than they wanted an instantaneous response.

Principle 5: Give People Rituals, and Stick to Them

Most service-encounter designers don't realize just how ritualistic people are. They find comfort, order, and meaning in repetitive, familiar activities. Rituals are particularly important in longer-term, professional-service encounters: they're used to mark key moments in the relationship, establish professional credentials, create a feeling of inclusion, flatter customers, set expectations, and get feedback. Common rituals include glowing introductions of staff at the start of an engagement, kickoff dinners, elegant PowerPoint presentations, final celebrations, and formal presentations to the CEO (even though he or she may not have an interest in the project). Many rituals are so small in scale that they're hard to name. Nonetheless, they play an important part in customers' perceptions of the experience. When McKinsey consultants listen to clients, for example, they pepper pauses in the conversation with a characteristic, noncommittal "uh-huh, uh-huh" that somebody once labeled the "McKinsey grunt." Sounds silly, but clients notice when it's missing.

Behavioral researchers have observed that these rituals provide an implicit standard for evaluating service encounters. Deviation from them is often cited as the cause of a failure—particularly in professional services, where customers have difficulty evaluating precise causes and effects. Check in with customers after something's gone badly with a service engagement, and you'll find that this is quite true. "If Henry had covered the ten-step model on the new benefits system like Susan did for the old one, it wouldn't have flopped." (The new system didn't require the ten-step ritual; it failed for a constellation of other reasons.) Or, "The consultant wearing the string tie was off in his forecast by 10%." (The dress code violation had nothing to do with the consultant's technical skills.)

It's easy to laugh at those examples, and more generally to dismiss people's tendency to focus on deviations from norms and rituals when they're trying to explain a failure. But make no mistake, behavioral science clearly shows how critical rituals are in long-term relationships. Not getting the weekly call from the consultant on a project, not copying the CEO on a progress report,

The Right Remedy

HOW DO YOU MAKE up for a service-encounter error? Research on what customers perceive as a fair remedy suggests that the answer depends on whether it is an outcome error or a process error. A botched task calls for material compensation, while poor treatment from a server calls for an apology. Reversing these recovery actions is unlikely to be effective.

Imagine being a copy store manager faced with two complaining customers. One says that the job was done right but the clerk was surly. The other says that the clerk was pleasant, but when he got home he realized that his report was missing two pages, and he had to take it to a competitor near his house to get the job done right. What should you do? In the case of the rude clerk, don't give the customer some tangible compensation, such as a coupon for his next visit. All the customer really wants is a sincere apology from the clerk and the manager. In the case of the botched job, you can apologize all over the place, but that won't satisfy the customer. He wants the job done right, and he wants some compensation for his inconvenience. Thus, while apologies are appropriate in both situations, behavioral research clearly indicates that process-based remedies should be applied to process-based problems and outcome-based remedies should be applied to outcome-based problems.

not returning phone calls immediately—any of these lapses can be blamed after the fact for a failure. They can also, and even more ominously, shift a customer's perceptions about the quality of the service, the service providers, and the company they represent.

Ultimately, only one thing really matters in a service encounter—the customer's perceptions of what occurred. Executives who design and oversee service encounters need to focus far more of their attention on the underlying factors affecting those perceptions. We believe that service encounters can be engineered to enhance the customer's experience during the process and his or her recollection of the process after it is completed.

We've used science to explore those factors, but you'll need to use your imagination to bring them alive. Put yourself in your customers' shoes and imagine their journey. Visualize every moment they spend with you and your employees. Which of their encounters should be lengthened? Which should be shortened? Where in a process are distractions most effective? Where should you offer choice to the customer? Which process rituals should not be violated? What are the last images of your service that customers take away, and how can you enhance them?

Behavioral science, applied with equal doses of empathy and imagination, can improve service delivery. More important, it can change the impressions that your customers remember, refer back to, and pass on to future customers.

Note

1. R. T. Mills and D. S. Krantz, "Information, Choice, and Reactions to Stress: A Field Experiment in a Blood Bank with Laboratory Analogue," *Journal of Personality and Social Psychology*, 1979.

RICHARD B. CHASE is the Justin Dart Professor of Operations Management at the University of Southern California's Marshall School of Business. **SRIRAM DASU** is an associate professor at the Marshall School.

Originally published in June 2001. Reprint R0106D

Best Face Forward

by Jeffrey F. Rayport and Bernard J. Jaworski

HOW DO YOU SERVE YOUR customers? Let us count the ways. You serve them through your retail stores, through your Web site, through your catalog and customer service call centers. You serve them through touch points that are human, like clerks and concierges, and you serve them through touch points that are automated, like vending machines and voice response units. If yours is like most companies, it has a broad collection of these interfaces and is investing in even more. But what it probably doesn't have is an interface system. That is to say, all of those ways you connect and interact with customers don't add up to an integrated and unique capability to manage relationships.

Unless you manage it explicitly for advantage, that portfolio of interfaces is going to become your biggest liability. Too many people and too many machines operating with insufficient coordination (and often at cross-purposes) will mean rising complexity, costs, and customer dissatisfaction. Turning that liability into a competitive asset is possible—indeed, it's what will separate the winners from the losers in practically every industry sector. But realizing new levels of effectiveness and efficiency will require a serious reengineering effort.

Perhaps in the context of the front office the term "reengineering" is surprising. Since it took the business world by storm in the 1990s, the approach has usually been applied to behind-the-scenes operations. But reengineering's principles—starting with a clean slate, redesigning processes in light of current capabilities— are strikingly suited to today's front office. Every indication, whether it be declining customer satisfaction indexes or the actions of the typical retail employee, signals that the customer interface is ripe for reinvention. At the same time, the rapid evolution of what we call "interface technologies" is making the reinvention of frontline service interactions—and of the entire service sector—possible.

Reengineering the front office will probably not be much easier than reengineering the back office. In some respects it will be harder. But consider the alternative. Your interface system is ultimately the face your company presents to customers and markets. Can you afford not to put your best face forward?

The Interface Imperative

The truth is that interactions with customers, and the customer experiences that result from those interactions, are, for many businesses, the sole remaining frontier of competitive advantage. If this seems to overstate the point, consider the four broad trends that have brought us to this watershed.

Idea in Brief

In this age of commoditization, new products and services become generic faster than ever. Your company can no longer count on innovative offerings to create sustainable success. The final frontier of competitive advantage? The quality of customers' experiences with your company. Consider this research finding: Service quality carries five times more weight in influencing purchase decisions than a product's features, performance, and even price.

But most companies serve their customers through flawed interfaces: too many people and too many machines—store clerks, Web sites, catalogs, call centers, voice response devices—often operating at cross purposes. Result? Rising complexity, costs, and customer dissatisfaction.

How to perfect your service quality—and leave rivals behind? Organize your customer interfaces into one coordinated system. Then ensure that the system's components work together to create satisfying experiences for customers *every* time they interact with your firm.

By combining the unique strengths of people (conveying empathy, handling exceptions) and technology (performing rote tasks, processing information), top-notch customer interface systems give each customer what he wants— whether it's efficiency, information, advice, social contact, or anonymity.

When you crack the code of successful customer interface systems, your customers view *your* service as more valuable than your rivals'. And you take a crucial step toward owning the competitive future.

First of all, competitive differentiation along traditional dimensions of corporate performance is becoming largely unsustainable. Ours is an era of near total commoditization. Several years ago, consumer electronics executives in Taiwan developed the habit of using the English phrase "three-six-one" to refer to the competitive dynamics of their business. What they

Idea in Practice

In exceptional customer interface systems, the interfaces (whether human or machine) succeed along four dimensions:

- **Physical presence and appearance:** The Four Seasons Hotel boasts a uniformed, clean-cut, businesslike, and courteous frontline staff.

- **Knowledge:** Amazon's Web site has encyclopedic knowledge of the company's enormous stock, seemingly perfect recall of what customers purchased in the past, and the ability to make well-informed recommendations.

- **Emotion:** Southwest's flight crews use humor to add emotional value to travelers' experience.

- **Connectivity:** Amazon's user community enables customers to tap into each other's experiences to select products.

To create a customer interface system that meets these criteria:

Understand your customers' desired experiences. Customers in different situations want different things from an interface. Fit your service interactions to suit customers' preferences.

> *Example:* One customer filling a prescription at a pharmacy might want hand-holding by the pharmacist; another, privacy through anonymity. An astute pharmacist treats the first customer with warmth and concern; the second, with efficiency and reserve.

Leverage technology's strengths. In many service settings, machines outperform human beings in managing interactions and relationships. Invest in technologies that

meant was three months to create a feature, function, and price configuration that differentiated an offering in consumer markets; six months to harvest the margin afforded by that differentiation; and one month to liquidate excess inventory after the offering became a commodity. A ten-month product life cycle! Such compensate for people's short-comings.

Example: Some hotels offer lobby kiosks that enable customers to check themselves in and out, get room keys and billing statements, upgrade rooms, leave messages for other guests, and print boarding passes. Customers get accurate, efficient service; the hotels cut personnel costs.

Decide where service work should be done. Some service work is more accurately performed remotely. For instance, McDonald's realized that fast-food drive-through clerks record 50%+ of orders incorrectly owing to distracting noise from food-service operations. The company placed drive-through operators in remote, centralized call centers, where operators manage order taking for several restaurants simultaneously.

Optimize performance across your system. Customers using multiple channels to buy from you (store, catalog, Web site) spend four times as much as single-channel users. To capitalize on these customers' economic potential, simplify interfaces that confuse or impede customers in the buying process. Give the lion's share of your attention and resources to interfaces your customers use most.

Example: TV-shopping network QVC invested heavily in the Web in South Korea, where high-levels of broadband penetration of Korean homes put the Web (enhanced by streaming video) ahead of television broadcasts as the company's most heavily used customer interface.

abbreviated life cycles have infected nearly every industry (partly as a result of the diffusion of electronics itself into every sector of the economy), making new offerings generic or obsolete faster than ever before. Sector after sector in the economy suffers from over-capacity. And margins, even for highly sophisticated technology products, are difficult to maintain. For most businesses in most industries, the opportunities to create sustainable offerings-based advantages are few and far between—or simply nonexistent.

Second, there is longstanding evidence that quality of service matters very much to customers—in many cases, much more than price or performance. One large-scale research study spanning consumer and industrial businesses, for example, measured the role of service quality in customers' decisions to switch vendors. The variables the researchers examined were service quality, product features and functions, performance, and price. The results showed that service quality had five times more weight in influencing purchase and repurchase decisions than any other attribute tested.

Third, given the greatly expanded scope of service work in the economy, finding appropriately skilled labor is getting harder and harder. In most developed countries today, the vast majority of jobs are service oriented and involve interaction with customers. Recent data from the U.S. Bureau of Labor Statistics indicate that over 90% of workers in industrialized economies are employed in service positions. Back when frontline employees represented a small proportion of the total workforce, it was easier for companies to fill customer-facing jobs with cream-of-the-crop talent. Companies trying to staff their front lines today are dipping much deeper into the labor pool, tapping less skilled workers. Airlines, hotels, and retailers of all stripes have a notoriously hard time recruiting and retaining motivated and presentable individuals for frontline positions. Consider fast food. Franchises recruit high school students, who spend an average of four or five months in these jobs. The low-skill workforces that fast-food franchises field have an annual turnover of 138%. This is a big part of why corporate America spends $50 billion a year on the remedial education of its workers. To be effective in customer-facing roles, employees must be literate and numerate and, ideally, have analytic capabilities, well-honed interpersonal skills, and emotional intelligence. The cost of such talent will only escalate as the baby boom generation ages and exits the workforce and demand for such labor grows.

Finally, new forms of interface technology are emerging that can assist frontline employees or stand in for them in customer-facing roles. Over decades, we have seen a gradual encroachment of machines upon traditionally human tasks involved in delivering services, managing relationships, and interacting with customers. Customers have become more and more comfortable dealing with machines through interactions with companies' offerings, and the technology inherent in those machines has advanced. Machines are proving to be viable alternatives not merely for processing rote transactions but for managing human interactions in sophisticated and unprecedented ways.

If you've been to an REI store, for example, you've probably seen one such innovation, interactive kiosks, in action. The kiosks augment the sporting goods stores' available SKUs (which number about 30,000) by allowing customers to order from a catalog of more than 78,000 items. More important, they also augment the sales clerks' knowledge of product features, comparative strengths, and recommended uses—and thus the company's ability to serve customers effectively. As one manager put it, "No matter how smart [our store clerks] are, they can't keep 45,000 pages of information [in their heads]." Supermarkets like Kroger have gone a different route with self-checkout stations. U-Scan and Fast Lane installations, which cost about $100,000 for a four-lane setup, give customers a faster checkout option; they also save the grocer money (because all four lanes are under the watchful eye of just one human cashier). Rite Aid is trying to achieve the same kind of leverage for its pharmacists, especially in light of a foreseeable workload crisis. Prescription orders are expected to rise at least 26% between 2001 and 2005, while the number of available pharmacists in the workforce will increase by less than 4%. So Rite Aid is experimenting with voice response units to process phone orders and robots to dispense medications, enabling its pharmacists to concentrate on developing higher quality relationships with customers.

The Four Dimensions of an Interface

A service interface is any place at which a company seeks to manage a relationship with a customer, whether through people, technology, or some combination of the two. Be it human or machine, every service interface must deliver high levels of customer-perceived value relative to the competition, so that customer satisfaction and loyalty rise sufficiently to drive superior financial returns. To deliver that level of value, an interface must succeed along four different dimensions: physical presence and appearance, cognition, emotion or attitude, and connectedness. At the Four Seasons Hotel, the appearance of frontline staff—uniformed, clean-cut, businesslike, courteous, individual, and authentic—is a physical differentiation. At Nordstrom, the average salesperson's ability to recognize and reward the store's best customers with appropriate service and attention is a cognitive advantage. The sense of humor and energy that Southwest's flight crews display add value on an emotional dimension. And the coordinating communications that allow the Four Seasons' staff to orchestrate a seamless hospitality experience, that enable Nordstrom's salespeople to transfer customers gracefully from one department to the next, and that make it possible for Southwest's crews to work as a team in flight are forms of connectedness that make a difference.

As you work to reengineer your front office, your goals should be to bring your various, proliferating customer interfaces into a coherent, optimized system, while ensuring that each interface, through the right use of people, machines, or a combination of both, succeeds on all of these dimensions. This is not simply a variation on the old theme of "high tech/high touch" in which number crunching and other rote tasks are automated to free up humans to make deeper customer connections. That dichotomy is no longer valid; now high-tech and high-touch can, and do, go hand in hand, with machines in some situations outperforming human workers in creating high-touch experiences for customers.

The Front-Office Revolution

When Tom Davenport and Michael Hammer (in separate articles) defined the concept of reengineering back in 1990, what they were urging us to do was rethink the design of operations in light of new IT capabilities. Too often they saw managers using computers to automate existing processes and roles in order to get work done incrementally faster. Greater gains, they showed, would come from focusing on the strengths of emerging and evolving technologies and radically redesigning business processes and roles to exploit them.

Front-office reengineering does exactly that. It uses new forms of technology to change the shape of customer interaction and relationship management functions. At the same time, it goes well beyond the first reengineering movement's aim to make a company "easier to do business with" through improvements in internal organizational processes. The focus now is on such arrestingly human concerns as the personal, aesthetic, and emotional attributes of customer interactions—none of which was even contemplated by reengineering as it was originally conceived. In its most thorough form, front-office reengineering subjects every current and potential service interface to an analysis of opportunities for *substitution* (deploying machines instead of people), *complementarity* (deploying combinations of machines and people), and *displacement* (using networks to shift physical locations of people and machines) with the twin objectives of compressing costs and driving top-line growth through increased customer-perceived value. In the subsections that follow, we offer the outlines of a front-office reengineering project, with some of the considerations that should inform each step.

Understand the desired customer experience

Customers in different situations want different things from an interface: information, advice, social exchange, affirmation, anonymity, discretion, and sometimes simply efficiency. The best starting point for front-office reengineering is an analytic understanding of the needs and desires of all segments of your customers, taking into account purchase occasions as well as competitive offerings. First, envision the appropriate customer experiences; then you can work backward to the interactions and relationships that shape those experiences and ultimately to the configuration of the customer interfaces that will successfully mediate those relationships.

It's important to understand that this is not customer relationship management as the field of CRM has defined it. CRM is commonly used to refer to large-scale enterprise software systems designed to manage customer information for sales and service. What we're talking about is more comprehensive—everything a company does to interact with, or relate to, the customers and markets that its strategy aims to serve.

Depending on the customer and the purchase occasion, what constitutes an appropriate experience may vary dramatically. We personally discovered this when we undertook some field research by working an evening shift at a Boston-area McDonald's. Customers who came to the drive-through had no interest in relating to a human being (much as we tried greeting them exuberantly as they drove up). Rather, they wanted an efficient transaction that met certain functional criteria, like speed, accuracy, and responsiveness. But walk-in customers wanted to relate to the real person behind the counter. (One apparent regular, a middle-aged man who looked as if he had spent too many years at high-tech start-ups, came in late. He eyed us suspiciously, placed his order hesitantly, then declared, "Something here is not normal. . . . It looks as if this McDonald's was taken over by Genuity!")

We learned a profound lesson here about personalization. Managers often believe that personalization only means affecting greater familiarity with a customer ("Hi, I'm Bob. I'll be your waiter today!"). But personalization should really be about custom-fitting service interactions to individual customers' preferences and even to individuals' varying needs in varying circumstances. One customer filling a prescription at a pharmacy counter might need some hand-holding by the pharmacist; another might want nothing more than privacy through anonymity. An astute pharmacist would provide "personalized" service by treating the first customer with warmth and concern and the second with reserve and efficiency. (Indeed, the first and second customer interactions may be with the same person on different days, dealing with different ailments.) We call this the *personalization paradox*—the notion that a personalized interaction or relationship may be one that is coldly impersonal.

The personalization paradox was no doubt the impetus behind Shop 2000, an experimental, fully automated vending machine that enabled customers to help themselves to typical convenience store items—even milk and eggs. Mind you, this wasn't introduced in a tough neighborhood in which the concern was for clerk safety. It was located in the fashionable Adams Morgan neighborhood of Washington, DC. But many of the machine's customers perceived it to be more accurate and reliable in executing transactions than a typical convenience store clerk—and refreshingly free of attitude. One commented, "A guy in the store can make a mistake or give you a hard time, but not the machine. I definitely prefer the machine."

Once you've understood what your customer requires from an interaction, you'll need to focus on what you, as a seller, want to gain from it—and how you might align your people and processes to deliver on those customer desires in a profitable manner. You might see the customer interaction as a chance to cross sell or up sell another offering, for example. You might want to use the opportunity to get feedback or do market research. It's vital to factor in these functions and to ensure they are given the right priority by the interface you deploy.

The experience of Sears offers a lesson here. In the 1990s, after divesting itself of its pioneering catalog operations and the Discover Card business, Sears chose to focus on delivering a differentiated customer experience in its brick-and-mortar stores. At one point in its much-publicized "turnaround" in the late 1990s, managers surveyed the company's retail workforce, some 300,000 frontline employees, to assess their grasp of the business and their role in its success. The stunning finding was that most employees reported that they were paid "to protect the assets of the company" from its customers. That response was wrongheaded; the whole point of displaying goods on a sales floor is to allow customers to interact with them. It was also wrong hearted; retailers can't succeed when their employees view the customer as the enemy.

Understand the potential of technology

At the same time that you're outlining what your interface system needs to accomplish, it's important to understand the current capabilities of technology. As in traditional reengineering, evolving technology drives efficiency, certainly—but the key to front-office reengineering is the realization that today's technology is also capable of taking on new and unprecedented roles with respect to managing interactions and relationships. Interestingly, our analysis of customer-facing technologies shows they are evolving rapidly along four lines—neatly mapped to the four dimensions of a successful interface. (See the exhibit "Interfacing with Machines.") We are seeing the proliferation of smart devices, the rising intelligence and interactivity of those devices, their increasing capacity to appeal on emotional levels, and the synaptic connectivity that links such devices to other devices and networks.

Interfacing with machines

Any good customer interface succeeds along four different dimensions—the physical, the cognitive, the emotional, and the synaptic. When machines can excel with respect to several of these simultaneously, the opportunity to reengineer the interface becomes an imperative.

Dimension	How machines are making inroads
Physical On the scene in sufficient numbers; presentable in appearance	**Ubiquity and pervasiveness of appealing, intelligent devices** Look around: Everywhere you'll see mobile phones, BlackBerrys, Palm devices, Pocket PC–based devices, MP3 players, high-tech wristwatches, and ever smaller and more powerful laptops.
Cognitive Able to recognize patterns, draw intelligent conclusions, and communicate articulately	**Exponentially increasing processing power** Intel says it's on track to double processing power every two years through 2011. New transistor insulators, such as strontium titanate, may sustain that momentum even longer.
Emotional Respectful; attentive; displaying brand-consistent personality attributes; emotionally calibrated with the customer	**Greater affective appeal to humans** A creature called Kizmet at the MIT Media Lab can read facial expressions through visual sensors, listen to words, and respond with facial expressions of its own in socially appropriate and emotionally valid ways.
Synaptic Well-connected to other resources important to the customer's experience	**Near ubiquitous global connectivity of information networks** High-speed broadband connectivity now exists in 70% of South Korean homes, resulting in a market where just about every device is easily connected by wire or wirelessly to every other. TiVo maintains periodic connectivity with its corporate servers, reporting consumer usage data, updating billing information, and generating programming recommendations.

We are already at the point that, in many service contexts, a machine may be able to outperform a human along any one of these lines. Amazon's Web site is a good example. Physically, it is as nearby as your desktop. Its graphic design presents a clean and accessible image, attentively, but not aggressively, awaiting your instructions. Its cognitive strengths are even greater. Unlike the typical person working in a shop, it has encyclopedic knowledge of its enormous stock, a seemingly perfect recollection for what you have purchased in the past, and the ability to make often well-informed recommendations. Even on an emotional level the site succeeds, with cheerful greetings and opinionated reviews. Perhaps more important, it's never in a bad mood, never short with dithering or demanding customers. And the site's user community provides a rich sense of connectivity. As you consider a purchase, you can tap into other buyers' experiences to guide you. If it's a rare book you seek, the site checks with every used book dealer in its virtual town (the so-called zShops).

It isn't only in online contexts that machines hold advantages. Think about the very unvirtual experience of travel, which is being transformed by a variety of self-service technologies. Delta—like nearly every other major airline—now allows customers to bypass the line at the counter and check in through ticketing kiosks; and, at United, you can do this in multiple languages, including English, French, and Spanish. Hertz allows gold-card members to pick up their assigned cars without a service representative's assistance. And if they need directions, customers can use NeverLost navigation systems in the cars to guide them while driving or kiosks at the Hertz stations to request and print them. The hotel chain Club Quarters enables members to check themselves in and out through an ATM-like machine in the lobby; it generates room keys and billing statements. Hilton, Sheraton, and Marriott are also installing kiosks to perform similar functions across their expansive chains to check guests in and out, upgrade rooms, leave messages for other guests, and, through partnerships with airlines, print boarding passes. And ATMs allow you to get local currency in most any city. A *Wall Street Journal* piece summed up the trend: "How to Have a Pleasant Trip: Eliminate Human Contact."

As such innovations steadily emerge to make our lives easier, it may not be obvious how revolutionary they are. The display technology itself is only part of the story. Never before have so many large-scale enterprises across so many industry sectors possessed the technological infrastructures or networks to deploy front-office machines like these. These resources are the result of decades of sustained investment in information technology in major corporations. Increasingly ubiquitous networks and technology diffusion link those corporations to consumers. And, as we discuss in the sidebar "Touchy Subjects," the new front-office machines are making inroads in even that most human of attributes—emotional connection.

Match the interface type to the task

Depending on the kinds of interaction called for, a particular service interface might preferably be people-dominant, machine-dominant, or a hybrid of the two.

Touchy Subjects

AT THE DAWN OF industrial automation more than a century ago, it became the goal of many managers to train factory workers to behave like machines. Getting employees on the plant floor to adapt their actions to the technologies of industrial production was the key to making lines run faster. Time-and-motion studies became the driver of a new frontier of industrial productivity.

Today, competition is arguably based far more on the quality of customer interactions with companies than on the efficiency of companies' processes. So as we move machines into frontline roles, we now must train machines to act more like people.

According to computer scientist Hans Moravec, the evolution of machine intelligence can be thought of in biological terms. Today's lawn-mowing and vacuuming robots belong to what he considers the first generation of development. They can perform simple tasks, but they can't adapt to changing circumstances. Within a decade, a second-generation robot with the cognitive capacity of a mouse will respond to positive and negative reinforcement within predefined circumstances, allowing it to improve its performance substantially over time. By 2040, Moravec expects third-generation robots with monkey-like intelligence to be capable of learning quickly from "mental rehearsals" involving simulations of physical, cultural, and psychological factors. In other words, such machines will have a primitive kind of consciousness. Through exposure to simulations of everyday situations, the robots will be trained to operate in the world and can then be retuned to stay "faithful to reality." By 2050, Moravec foresees fourth-generation "universal robots" that can "abstract and generalize [and] become intellectually formidable."

What's interesting is that, even though we are today living only in the first generation, with glimpses of the second, it is clear that machines are already eliciting emotional responses in humans once reserved for other people or household pets. As well as being able to tell one person from another (and respond to them differently), AIBO, Sony's "entertainment robot" that resembles a small dog, develops its own unique personality. The product is endowed with 16,000 latent personality attributes, which are activated, or not, through interactions with its owner. As a result, many owners reportedly develop a conviction that AIBO is alive. They give their AIBOs names and refer to them not as "it" but as he or she. They talk about them not as "robots" or "toys" but as dogs or other pets and take them to AIBO clinics, AIBO birthday parties, and AIBO soccer matches. This is a level of emotional attachment that does not normally accrue to, say, a microwave oven or a digital camera.

TiVo, the system that allows people to digitally record favorite television shows and skip over the ads on playback, elicits other emotionally charged responses. Because the machine learns enough from past viewing selections to make program recommendations, there have been reports of people being concerned about "what my TiVo thinks of me"—and purposely viewing or storing content to alter its opinion of them.

We can only speculate on the emotional bonds that will develop once Mitsubishi Heavy Industries puts its new household robot Wakamaru on the market (expected this year). Designed to provide companionship for older people, it recognizes individual faces and 10,000 spoken words, conveys news from the Internet, and engages in prolonged conversations. Perhaps even more advanced, Toyota's "partner robot" features lips designed to "move with the same finesse as human lips" (as its Web site announces).

Robotics is just one stream of technology that marries high-tech with high-touch. It promises to radically alter the organizational models for how companies serve their customers—and to transform the enterprise economics of companies. Just as business was incredulous that steam-powered turbines could drive textile mills in the late nineteenth century at lower costs with higher-quality output, many today are unconvinced that machines can manage customer interactions and relationships in credible, customer-satisfying, and loyalty-inducing ways. But it's a fact that machines are beginning, for better or worse, to play or restructure such roles and are encroaching on a sacred precinct of human activity.

Which type of interface to use at each given touch point is a strategic choice that has related costs and customer outcomes. A waiter in a restaurant, for example, constitutes a people-dominant service interface (even if supported by computerized ordering systems). A vending machine or a Web site is a machine-dominant service interface (even if supported by people for maintenance and development). Call centers, which are staffed by people who cannot perform their jobs without access to database systems, are hybrid service interfaces. Deciding which of these interface types will allow you to best manage customer interactions and relationships is, first, a matter of determining what people do best and what machines do best—the new division of labor.

The idea that people and machines bring different performance capabilities to the labor force has emerged in recent years as a focus of academic inquiry. MIT professor Erik Brynjolfsson, for instance, has proposed a preliminary catalog of human and machine strengths, where humans excel in "judgment, pattern recognition, exception processing, insight, and creativity" and machines excel in "collecting, storing, transmitting, and routine processing." Certainly this division of labor holds at major airports, where e-ticketing machines enable customers to purchase tickets, check themselves in on flights, and in some cases select their seat assignments—leaving the few remaining humans behind the counter to manage complex or problematic ticketing situations, communicate about delayed or canceled flights, and conduct security screening. But this represents a fairly traditional—and therefore limited—view of what machines can credibly and capably do.

The right combination of people and machines leverages the strengths of each. It also recognizes their weaknesses. People may be good at conveying empathy and handling exceptions, but they are challenging to manage and costly to deploy and train. Machines may be excellently suited to processing information and performing rote tasks, but they can depersonalize or homogenize interactions. In effect, the front office needs machines to compensate for people's shortcomings and people to compensate for machines'.

Relative costs, of course, must be considered in the optimal allocation of effort between people and machines. For example, it may be impossible for machines to beat skilled financial advisers at everything they do. But Charles Schwab was still wise to spend $20 million creating Schwab Equity Ratings, an automated online service that provides buy and sell recommendations for roughly 3,000 equities. Its stock picks are not necessarily better than those made by investment professionals, but they are of comparable quality. More to the point, the system conserves the energy of the organization's scarcest, least scalable asset—its skilled and empathetic people—so it can be applied where distinctly human capabilities and presence count most.

Trends in labor and technology costs suggest that machines will continue to encroach on the frontline territory now held by humans. Right now, for example, it costs companies $9.50 on average to respond in person to a telephone inquiry from a customer. Addressing the same customer live by e-mail costs $9.00. Meeting the customer's needs through online text chat, where one representative can handle several customers at once, costs $5.00. Handling the interaction using e-mail by a live person with automated assists or macros costs $2.50. And if the interaction is fully automated, the savings are even more dramatic. An interactive voice response unit can handle the inquiry for just $1.10 if it does not default to a human being; a Web site can handle it for $0.50; and an automated e-mail response unit, if suitable, can handle it for just $0.25. When you consider that the world's call centers were handling 26 billion call minutes a month by mid-2003—with projections of 35 billion call minutes a month by 2007—it's hard to overestimate the economic impact of this kind of front-office automation.

To the extent that we see robotics on the front line, its potential is even greater. According to *World Robotics 2003*, a report by the International Federation of Robotics and the United Nations, if you index the price of robots and the cost of human labor with 1990 as the baseline, the robot price index has decreased from 100 to 36.9 (or to 18.5 if you adjust for the higher performance quality of today's robots) while the index for human labor compensation has risen from 100 to over 151. What does all this mean? Simply that people-dominant interfaces, which have long prevailed in traditional frontline services, are no longer the only or obvious choice at every point of connection between companies and their customers. As technology continues to evolve and customers become more comfortable with it, machine-dominant interfaces will inevitably become more prominent on the front lines of many businesses, and capable people—because of their increasing scarcity and cost—will inevitably ascend to higher order roles and responsibilities.

Put work in its (right) place

If you think, to borrow from Tip O'Neill, that all service is local, you may need to think again. Reengineering the front office also involves choices between performing services proximally (in stores, for example) or remotely (through network connections to customers or operations off-site).

Think, for example, about utility meter reading, which is now commonly done over wireless networks. The meters report directly to utility companies on power usage, making it unnecessary for employees to drive from house to house and collect the information manually. It's one of the better-known examples of network-based machine-to-machine communication, but tens of millions of other devices substitute for people in similar ways. One company, BioLab, is even using remote machines to supervise the work of people. A supplier of swimming pool chemicals, BioLab has developed a system of remote sensors to keep watch over the water quality of its clients' pools. The sensors send data across the cellular network to the company, and if they report a chemical imbalance, the company's system calls or pages the client's designated maintenance person. If that person takes no action, the system contacts the next person up the chain of command (the maintenance person's boss) until the problem is resolved.

Remote work can, of course, also be performed by remote humans. One of the most striking examples we've encountered is in staffing for fast food drive-through windows. From an operating perspective, this fix is long overdue. Drive-through clerks in restaurants are stationed amid noisy food service facilities, and an industry survey recently revealed that, on average, more than half of the orders they take are recorded incorrectly. So why not place these drive-through operators in a remote, centralized call center so that they can manage order-taking for several restaurants at once? That's exactly what some franchises are now piloting. Today, you can use the drive-through at a McDonald's in Missouri and place an order with a call center clerk in Colorado—nearly a thousand miles away. Increasingly, we will see companies leaning toward such distant gratification. (For a best practice example, see the sidebar "I've Never Seen Them, but I Believe They Exist.")

Pushing front-office work offshore has obvious, if politically divisive, allure. Bank of America has said it can perform work that costs $100 an hour in the United States for $20 an hour in India. At one Indian call center, operated by Spectramind (a unit of the giant Indian systems integrator Wipro), a highly skilled customer service representative with a college degree earns an annual income of $3,710, nearly an order of magnitude less than the going rate in the United States. By early 2003, Spectramind employed 4,000 people, many of whom received voice and accent training to work effectively with North American consumers, while working in call centers that surrounded them physically with the arcana of American popular sports and music culture.

Obviously there are cost-compression benefits. But the larger issue here is that ubiquitous networks and proliferating devices create new strategic choices for managers. Making the choices correctly depends on understanding what people and machines can do separately and together, whether they should be physically proximal to or can be remote from the customer interaction, and then determining what attributes (in cost and customer outcomes) deserve what levels of relative priority.

Optimize performance across the system

An important challenge in front-office reengineering is not only optimizing interfaces individually but also optimizing them, in concert, as a system. You could argue that some of your customers don't require such optimization, because they access your products or services through only one or two touch points or channels. While that's true, a preponderance of evidence suggests that such customers are the least valuable to your business. Multichannel customers—who interact or shop across multiple interfaces—are most engaged with company brands, spend more on the brands, and are the drivers of growth in revenues and profitability. (Recent retailing data suggest that customers using three or more channels—such as store, catalog, and online—spend four times as much as single-channel customers, and they represent the most rapidly changing aspect of consumer

I've Never Seen Them, but I Believe They Exist

FIRST DIRECT IS THE PIONEERING direct bank that has amassed arguably the world's most loyal banking customers by effectively deploying one of the most satisfying service interfaces in the financial services sector. Headquartered in Leeds, the company began in 1989 as a wholly owned subsidiary of Midland Bank, then one of the Big Four national banks in the United Kingdom. Midland Bank had never been a market leader in terms of customer service; in fact, surveys showed it was the most-hated bank in England. It had only a small segment of extremely satisfied account holders alongside more than 10 million dissatisfied ones. And why were these few hundred thousand souls so satisfied? Because they never entered a branch.

These individuals had pieced together their own interface systems in interacting with Midland Bank, combining telephone, ATM, and Royal Mail. Most met with their branch manager only when they had problems. Otherwise, they used remote channels. Predictably, this segment was younger, better educated, more technologically savvy, and concentrated disproportionately in professional jobs, with significantly better earning prospects than the general population. These account holders did not maintain the highest bank balances, but they also did not require a great deal of attention. In terms of customer lifetime value, this segment was without question among the most profitable.

Thus, First Direct was born—before any other bank in the world had attempted to operate without a brick-and-mortar, branch-based model. The bank cultivated a new kind of employee, called the "banking representative" (BR), to deal with customers exclusively over the phone. BRs were people who had certain "life skills" but had never worked in any of the Big Four banks. The recruits, mostly women taking a few years off from their careers as lawyers, accountants, and business managers to care for children, needed jobs with flexible hours.

Each BR was equipped with a PC workstation that could access the bank's customer information systems, which provided three levels of information on account holders. They tracked customers' *identity* data—name, address, phone number, age, and income;

how they came to the bank; and when they opened their account. They also tracked histories of customer accounts, such as deposits, withdrawals, transfers, changes of job or address, and past purchases of banking products or services. Though most banks viewed such histories as transactional, First Direct considered them *behavioral,* a source of insight into customers' future needs and desires. And the systems collected *emotional* data, such as a BR's observations of a customer's moods, personality, and disposition, which enabled other BRs to interact with the callers according to each customer's preferences and individual style. At the start of each call from a returning customer, the system signaled not only what to discuss but also how to discuss it.

First Direct provided no means of face-to-face interaction between employees and customers, and it acknowledged its abstract nature in several early TV spots. (In one TV commercial, an articulate, elegant man sat near a fireplace sipping tea; after a few seconds, he looked up at the camera and, as if sharing a revelation, said, "I've never seen the people at First Direct, but I believe—*I believe!*—they exist.") Also, unlike other direct-banking firms, First Direct did not assign specific BRs to particular customers. In fact, its capacity to provide personal service on demand depended on routing incoming calls to any of hundreds of BRs regardless of who had handled prior interactions. No customer would be likely to speak to the same BR twice in the course of a typical multiyear banking relationship. Yet, when we asked customers to describe their dealings with First Direct, many claimed it was the most personal relationship they had ever had with a financial institution—or, for that matter, with any large business.

By the early 1990s, First Direct was the United Kingdom's fastest-growing bank and the only one with significant brand equity. It had achieved customer satisfaction rates above 90% and nearly perfect levels of account retention. It went on to qualify at the top of the UK banking industry's customer satisfaction rankings for twelve years (and counting), starting in 1991. When accounts were closed, it tended to be for one of two reasons. Either the account holder was moving out of the United Kingdom (the bank's only market) or that person had died.

retail behavior.) Interface systems must be optimized in order to capitalize on the economic potential of these customers. To do so, we advise managers to focus on this sequence of activities: separate, relate, and integrate. In the *separate* phase, companies should focus on reengineering individual interfaces to improve their performance while lowering operational cost wherever feasible. This phase focuses on individual interface performance: How effective is a customer service representative in a call center, a sales clerk in a retail store, a Web site online?

In the *relate* phase, companies should determine what the "anchor" interfaces in the customer experience are based on observation of customer usage and how customers' buying processes will flow from those points across the system. In every interface system, some interfaces matter more than others. Customers may use one with great frequency but use another one for longer durations. These interfaces must receive management's highest priority for attention and resources. Similarly, in every interface system, customers can flow down one or more logical paths, based on how customers interact in the relevant buying processes. A company cannot optimize an interface system without understanding anchor interfaces and customer flows. For example, managers at TV-shopping network QVC know that the televised broadcast is their anchor interface and that customer traffic largely flows along a dominant pathway through the system—from the broadcast to the phone, voice response unit, or online site, and then to order placement and fulfillment. But they also know that shoppers are increasingly using the

Web as the anchor interface (for example, while they're at work and don't have access to a television) and order online, never watching the broadcast or accessing the call centers. This is the case in South Korea, where high-speed broadband penetration of Korean homes has made the Web the anchor interface (enhanced by streaming video) ahead of the broadcast. Once a company has identified the dominant pathways through the buying process of its most profitable customers, it should optimize its interface system to handle those flows best, since they represent the highest priorities from a business performance perspective.

In the *integrate* phase, managers must focus on meshing interfaces and linkages to maximize effectiveness. That requires closing performance gaps—pain points (aspects of connection, either interfaces or linkages among interfaces within the system, that dissatisfy customers in the buying process), choke points (points that confuse or impede customers in the buying process), and drop-off points (points that result, through pain or confusion, in customer defections from the buying process)—while amplifying operational efficiencies. Here, it's useful to keep in mind the wisdom of Albert Einstein and make everything as simple as possible, but not simpler. Interface systems have a natural tendency to grow more complex over time. Many companies either add interfaces or elaborate on existing ones in response to customer demand and their own opportunities for innovation. But having too many interfaces in a system is as deleterious to the quality of a company's customer interactions as too few.

About Face

As the focus of competition shifts from *what* companies do to *how* they do it, the new frontier of competitive advantage lies in the quality of interactions and relationships companies can establish with their customers and markets. So it is indeed fortunate that frontline service is undergoing a revolution of its own. Advances in service technology have opened up new possibilities for how companies can create value not only through improvements in productivity but through better interactions with their customers.

Now with both motive and means, businesses must change fast to embrace these new realities. Reengineering the front office will eliminate and displace many jobs, but it will also inevitably create new opportunities for human labor. Getting the balance right will require business leaders to develop a subtle understanding of how to manage the intelligent division of labor between people and machines. A company's interface system works best when it combines the best of what people and machines can do. This task of managing interfaces and interface systems will prove to be a strategic imperative—perhaps *the* strategic imperative for many companies. Those who crack the code of interface systems will own the competitive future.

JEFFREY F. RAYPORT and **BERNARD J. JAWORSKI** are cofounders of Marketspace, a research and consulting unit of Monitor Group.

Originally published in December 2004. Reprint R0412B

Index